# SURROUNDED BY
# IDIOTS

Grateful acknowledgment is made to reprint the following:

Excerpt from the *Seattle Post-Intelligencer,* "Making Sense of the Debate About Hillary Clinton," by Andrew Alexander. © Cox News Service. Reprinted with permission.

Excerpt from the *Centre Daily Times,* "Gallagher 'Humbled' by Huge Turnout," by Nichole Dobo. © *Centre Daily Times.* Reprinted with permission.

Excerpt from *Insight on the News,* "NPR Sets Dial on Broadcasting Bias," by John Berlau. © The Associated Press. All rights reserved. Reprinted with permission.

Election 2004 map. © The Associated Press. All rights reserved. Reprinted with permission.

"Ode to Old Blue" lyrics, © Pete Baum. Reprinted with permission.

Excerpt from the *Boston Globe,* "Free to Marry Historic Date Arrives," by Yvonne Abraham and Rick Klein. © 2004 by Globe Newspaper Co (MA). Reproduced with permission of GLOBE NEWS-PAPER CO (MA) in the format Other Book via Copyright Clearance Center.

Excerpt from Associated Press interview with Rick Santorum. © The Associated Press. All rights reserved. Reprinted with permission.

Excerpt from "Gay Groups Ask Senate GOP to Reconsider Santorum Post" by Lara Lakes Jordan. © The Associated Press. All rights reserved. Reprinted with permission.

Excerpt from the *New York Times,* "Cosby Defends His Remarks About Poor Blacks' Values," by Felicia R. Lee. © 2005 The New York Times Co. Reprinted with permission.

Excerpt from "Stung by Anti-war Criticism, Hall Cancels *Bull Durham* Festivities," by Ben Walker. © The Associated Press. All rights reserved. Reprinted with permission.

HarperCollins books may be purchased for educational, business, or sales promotional use. For information please write: Special Markets Department, HarperCollins Publishers, 10 East 53rd Street, New York, NY 10022.

FIRST EDITION

*Designed by Kris Tobiassen*

Printed on acid-free paper

Library of Congress Cataloging-in-Publication Data

Gallagher, Mike.
    Surrounded by idiots : fighting liberal lunacy in America / by Mike Gallagher.—1st ed.
      p.   cm.
    ISBN 0-06-073798-0

    1. Liberalism—United States.   2. United States—Politics and government—2001–   I. Title.
JC574.2.U6G35   2005
320.51'3'0973—dc22                                     2005043413

05   06   07   08   09   DIX/QW   10  9  8  7  6  5  4  3  2  1

# SURROUNDED BY
# IDIOTS

## FIGHTING LIBERAL LUNACY IN AMERICA

# MIKE GALLAGHER

### WITH A FOREWORD BY SEAN HANNITY

*WM*

WILLIAM MORROW
*An Imprint of* HarperCollins*Publishers*

To Denise, whose love and support are the
greatest gifts that I could ever hope to receive

# CONTENTS

# FOREWORD

I consider it a great honor to be invited by my good friend and colleague Mike Gallagher to write the foreword to this book. Having gone through the process of authoring two books, I know the many challenges and hurdles that writing a book can bring. Mike's first effort is a home run and one that is certain to delight his fans and soon-to-become fans alike.

Mike and I began our mutual admiration society when we were both starting out in New York City radio at WABC-AM. A couple of Irish guys with big plans and dreams in the big city, we found we had much in common: strong and supportive wives, a passion for talk radio, and a strong faith that gave us the courage of our convictions to say what we believe on the airwaves.

No one roots harder for Mike Gallagher to continue his success story than me. I've watched him make the transition from a radio host in Albany, New York, to morning-drive voice on the nation's most listened-to talk station, WABC. I've seen him grow as he went from a local host on WABC into national syndication, forming his own syndication company with the backing of a group of enthusiastic investors, men and women who knew great talent when they heard it. I cheered for him as he and the investors sold their company to Salem Radio Network, allowing him to continue his ascent in the national radio scene working for Salem, an influential and well-respected broadcasting company. And I'm proud of his ever-growing role at Fox News Channel as a contributor and guest host, particularly when he fills in for me on *Hannity and Colmes*.

Mike's journey is the quintessential American success story. And that's serendipitous because Mike is the quintessential great American. Not only is his career path an inspirational example of achieving one's dreams, but he believes in everything that makes America great. He cherishes the role of police and firefighters, calling them the last true heroes. He defends the honor of our men and women in the military, with particular emphasis on the families who are left behind. This book will feature the story of why he formed his charitable foundation, Gallagher's Army, a way to honor the brave men and women of battle and their families. And he treasures his wife, Denise, and their four boys, a love story featured in this book that will touch the heart of everyone who reads it.

His story is one all of us can relate to. Putting aside our like-minded ideologies and philosophies, his lifetime of hard work, solid values, and love of God, family, and country is a truly uplifting tale.

Thankfully, Mike does a masterly job of weaving his remarkable life into the compelling social and political issues he writes about in *Surrounded by Idiots*. From the culture wars to the monumental 2004 election, he covers it all. He skewers liberal lunacy with a sharp tongue and a hearty laugh. He even takes us up close and personal to a now-infamous cocktail party where a certain Hollywood liberal, taken in by Mike's charm, lets loose with an ominous warning about what the loony liberals would like to do with yours truly. I'll bet "Lou Grant" never thought he'd find himself in my buddy Mike Gallagher's first book!

As the author of a pair of books which deal with the need to defeat liberalism and despotism, it's refreshing to read this book written by a great iconoclast like Mike. He shatters all illusions about any remaining wisdom or merit of today's brand of liberalism. Any doubts about his ability to do so will be eliminated when one reads his chapter on notable liberals like Michael Moore or his ongoing battle with groups like PETA. Even his admirable story of losing seventy pounds—and keeping it off—is rooted in the foundation of personal responsibility, not government or societal intervention, always a favorite of today's liberals.

*Surrounded by Idiots* exposes the many fallacies of liberals and anti-American voices in an often funny, candid, bright, and thoughtful way. Mike has an amazing ability to blend humor and honesty in this book that will take you on an eye-opening adventure about the line drawn in the sand between out-of-touch liberals and mainstream conservatives.

You'll greatly enjoy this book, whether you're a conservative who already sees the light or a liberal who might now begin to do so.

SEAN HANNITY
New York, New York
February 2005

# SURROUNDED BY
# IDIOTS

# INTRODUCTION
# THE FIGHT FOR OUR GREAT NATION'S SOUL

Okay, let me start by setting the record straight. The people who usually surround me are loving, caring, funny, smart and terrific. They are my family, friends, coworkers, radio listeners and TV viewers.

But outside of that group, a liberal idiocy surrounds us all. It threatens to destroy the values and lifestyles that millions of us cherish.

America is mired in an unprecedented cultural and political war. The left is trying to destroy the pillars of our great country. Their targets: every value and standard, principle and ideal, concept of God, family, honor, duty, country and decency that we hold dear. As a people we need help because our country is battling for her very soul, for patriotism, Judeo-Christian morals and strong families. Liberal lunatics have surrounded us with their agenda-driven ideology. It's time to fight back.

If the 2004 election is any indication, the tide is beginning to turn. Maintaining America's role as the greatest nation in the world means we must stay the course and fight the good fight.

Day after day, week after week, year after year, I sit in a sound-proof glass booth hosting a talk radio show that is listened to by over two million people a week. In front of me are a microphone and a phone bank full of blinking lights representing callers from across our country.

The callers, everyday remarkable Americans from Florida to Indiana, from Texas to California, express their frustration and heartbreak over this battle. I hear outrage from farmers and teachers, factory workers and bosses, stay-at-home moms and office-bound dads. They're angry over attempts to stop students from reciting the pledge of allegiance in schools. They're aggravated because politicians and judges act like we live in a crackpot dictatorship instead of a freedom-loving nation. They're hurt that we're protecting atheists and rock-worshippers while eroding the rights of the religious. Americans are sick of the left-leaning agenda championed by teachers, mouthed by TV anchors and glamorized by movie stars.

The voices of these furious Americans are starting to be heard, a low murmur revving into a collective roar.

# 1
# LIBERAL LOONS TO THE LEFT OF ME

"So what's it gonna be, Gallagher—do you want to introduce your wife to Hillary Clinton or not?"

Never have I been asked a more dastardly question.

My wife, Denise, is a beautiful, kind, sweet, big-hearted woman. She is my best friend, my soul mate. Rarely a day passes that I don't thank God for her. But nobody's perfect and my beloved wife has a flaw. It is a nagging, maddening defect that regularly threatens to make my head explode.

Denise is a Democrat.

I'm not sure why. Her parents, Curt and Mary, are proud Republicans from Ohio. They, too, are pained by their daughter's political leanings. Lord knows I've tried every argument and applied all my powers of persuasion to try and win her over.

She won't budge, though.

So we're both resigned to a dreary stalemate: in our household, our votes cancel each other out. We try to avoid talking about politics whenever possible. And we still manage to love each other very much.

When I first got a radio show in New York City in the fall of 1996, my agent was George Hiltzik, the grand poo-bah of talk radio agents. He's a fast-talking bear of a man with an infectious laugh, usually screaming into two cell phones pressed to each ear. I've always loved the guy.

Now in 2000, George's son, Matthew, was working for Hillary Clinton's New York Senate race. He offered to have Matthew introduce my wife to one of her heroines, the former first lady/current carpetbagger who wanted to become a U.S. senator. Knowing how much I love my wife, George reveled in the lousy position this placed me.

"Mike, Matthew will be delighted to make this happen for you," he said, chuckling. "Hillary is speaking at an event at a Midtown synagogue next week. He'll arrange for the two of them to meet afterward. C'mon, what terrific show material you'll have! So what's it gonna be, Gallagher—do you want to introduce your wife to Hillary Clinton or not?"

It would have been so easy to say no thanks and never tell Denise what she had missed. You can't feel deprived over something you never knew you had, right? But no, I was destined to suffer. I kept thinking how excited Denise would be if she could actually shake Madame Hillary's hand. I put my distaste and disdain for this power-hungry politician on a seesaw, balancing that with my love and affection for Denise. Up, down, up, down. You can figure out which side I chose. After all, I can complain about Hillary on the radio every day if I want; having a chance to make Denise that happy is rare.

If I were to pull this off, I wanted to make it a big surprise. After giving George the green light, I only told Denise that we were going someplace "special" where she would meet a "mystery guest." Always up for an adventure, she said, "great" and off we went.

When we arrived at the synagogue, I scanned the outside of the building: no signs indicating who was appearing there. So far, so good. Denise pointed excitedly at the security and advance men, in sunglasses and earpieces, standing outside. If she guessed the identity of the "mystery guest," she didn't say.

Inside the synagogue, George Hiltzik was grinning from ear to ear as he showed us to our reserved seats. Denise now saw security men with earpieces patrolling inside the synagogue, too. She started to think she might be meeting someone named Clinton, maybe not the Democratic candidate for U.S. Senate but perhaps the former president.

When Hillary came out to speak, the joyful look on Denise's face made it all worthwhile. She put her hands over her mouth, which she always does when excited, and stared at the woman soon to be elected New York's junior senator and—perish the awful thought—probably headed for a run for president one day.

After the speech, we waited in a back room to meet Mrs. Clinton. She strode right up to us with a big, broad grin. "Denise, it's so great to meet you. We really need to work on this husband of yours and bring him over to *our* side."

Lady, you're good.

Like her husband, Hillary Rodham Clinton can make the person she's speaking to feel like the most important person in the room. Aides obviously briefed her about Denise and me right before she met us, but her apparent familiarity and ease with us still made us feel like we were a bunch of long-lost friends.

While I will always dislike Hillary Rodham Clinton, for one brief moment on a memorable morning I appreciated her kindness toward my wife.

You can chalk it up to me having a bad day.

Liberals like Hillary Rodham Clinton have turned the Democratic Party into something that is barely recognizable from the Democratic Party of our parents. John F. Kennedy was defined as a liberal Democrat, and yet history confirms his true colors as a war hawk, a president not afraid to plunge ahead with military action when he felt it was necessary. He gambled and lost in the disastrous 1961 Bay of Pigs invasion of Cuba, which had relied on faulty intelligence. Still, despite this failure, Kennedy never wavered when it came to protecting America. When he learned that the Soviet Union was establishing nuclear missile launch sites in Cuba, he acted quickly. Who can forget his tough, bold televised speech when he told the American people and warned the Soviets that the United States would consider any missile "launched from Cuba against any nation in the Western Hemisphere as an attack by the Soviet Union on the United States, requiring a full retaliatory response upon the Soviet Union." Then he demanded they dismantle the missile sites and launched a naval blockade to prevent the delivery of any offensive weapons to Cuba. This showed the communists we meant business. After five tense days, Soviet premier Nikita Khrushchev blinked and withdrew the missiles and the world was spared a nuclear war.

Now, that's a president, a man who can take decisive action and stand by what he says.

Today's Democrat is more apt to sound like a pacifist rather than a bold warrior, ready to defend America against our aggressors. Today's Democrat doesn't even have the words "decisive" or "action" in his vocabulary. Today's Democrat is Bill Clinton.

He was a disgraceful president, only the second in our history whose improprieties were grave enough to get him impeached (the other was Andrew Johnson in 1868.) A great myth about the Clinton impeachment, one of the darkest chapters in U.S. history, was that it was only about his infidelity. His selfish and destructive behavior with intern Monica Lewinsky wasn't the act that got him impeached. It was the lawlessness of his lying under oath, suborning perjury and obstructing an investigation.

How many times have we heard people call Richard Nixon's Watergate scandal a "third-rate burglary?" His abuse of power in desperately trying to cover up his administration's role in the break-in forced him to resign in shame. So why is "a third-rate burglary" more monumental than deceiving the American people and defying our system of justice?

It saddens me to see Bill Clinton treated like the Democratic Party's glorified elder statesman. Is he really the best they have to offer? If so, what a sorry state their party is in. His tedious, voluminous memoir, *My Life,* was an instant best seller. He gets ovations and accolades wherever he goes, making barrels of cash for reciting one of his scripted speeches. Clearly, he's the ringmaster smack dab in the center ring of the Democratic Party circus.

Liberal Democrats seem to forget that he dishonored the presidency and embarrassed our country, subjecting Americans to a painful, ugly process that practically ground our federal government to a halt. Worst of all, his defiance and reckless behavior contributed to the moral decay that continues to corrupt our culture. How does a parent explain to a child or teen or even college student that Bill Clinton emerged from an impeached presidency to be treated like a rock star? Even impressionable, morally conflicted adults have been forced to face the obvious: Clinton got away with criminal behavior while serving as president of the United States.

Liberal Democrats worship Bill and Hillary Clinton because for many of them, morality is relative. Forget Bill's transgressions because he cares about people. Ignore his lies to his country and his wife and child because he wants health care for all.

Please.

One of the more popular bumper stickers seen during the Clinton years said simply, CHARACTER MATTERS. If the leader of the free world is morally bankrupt, what does it say about the nation he leads? Whatever the fiercest critics of George W. Bush have to say about him, they can't say he suffers from a lack of character.

Affection for Bill Clinton is a type of liberal idiocy that has gravely hurt our great nation. It's a blind, thoughtless acceptance of a former president who should be regarded as a disgraced man. And affection is even more misguided for the new Clinton comer, Hillary, herself also a best-selling author, not to mention an opportunistic carpetbagger.

When Hillary was first lady, she acted as if she were an elected official. She made the huge blunder of trying to single-handedly reform the nation's health care system. Many Americans were quite uncomfortable with the president's wife plunging in like that. Hillary wasn't on the ballot and Americans didn't vote for her.

In the April 3, 1994, issue of the *Albany* (N.Y.) *Times Union* the headline read, COMING TO TERMS WITH THE "PROPER" ROLE OF FIRST SPOUSE HILLARY CLINTON INVITES A BACKLASH. Reporter Ann McFeatters writes, "Four out of ten people say they view Hillary Clinton unfavorably, unusually high for a first lady."

In the true Clinton tradition, Madame Clinton has had her own share of controversy over the years. Take Vince Foster, for instance. This longtime Clinton aide apparently committed suicide in a Washington, D.C., area park in 1993, when he was deputy White House counsel. Much has been written about Foster's death, a favorite topic among conspiracy theorists. As the theory goes, Hillary and Foster were having an affair and the Clintons had him killed because he was going to spill that and other secrets.

To me, this murder theory seems far-fetched. Still, there have always been suspicions about Mrs. Clinton's actions immediately after Foster's death. In the January 15, 1996, issue of the *Seattle Post-Intelligencer,* Andrew Alexander writes,

> There have been discrepancies involving what happened in the aftermath of the 1993 suicide of Deputy White House counsel Vincent Foster, who was a close friend and law partner of Hillary Clinton. He had worked on Whitewater matters at the Rose Law Firm and was known to be concerned about suspected mismanagement of the White House travel office. A Secret Service agent has testified that on the night of the suicide, Hillary Clinton's chief of staff, Maggie Williams, removed what were sus-

pected of being Whitewater files from Foster's White House office. Williams denies it. In her *"20/20"* interview, Clinton said "there were no documents taken out of Vince Foster's office the night he died."

Who would you believe, a Secret Service agent who is sworn to defend our president and our country, or the Clintons?

Why would they be worried about Whitewater? To refresh your memory, allow me to quote Mr. Alexander again:

> [Hillary performed] legal work during the 1980s for the Madison Guaranty Savings and Loan, a Little Rock thrift that went bust. Madison invested heavily in real estate ventures that failed, causing the thrift to collapse at a cost to taxpayers of $60 million. One of those deals was a land development venture known as Whitewater. President Clinton and his wife were partners in Whitewater, along with James McDougal. He headed Madison, which financed the project. Investigators have found evidence that money from Madison was diverted improperly into Whitewater, but the probe has not linked the Clintons to the diversion.

God only knows what they were covering up. Hillary Clinton represents everything that's wrong with the Democratic Party. Maybe it's her relentless ambition and drive for power. Perhaps it's her willingness to stay married to a lying, cheating husband to preserve her power base. When she won the U.S. Senate seat in New York State, where she had never lived or worked, it seemed she would use that platform to run for president.

God help us when that happens.

★ ★ ★

There are liberals like Bill and Hillary Clinton who are driven by political ambition at any cost, and then there are liberals like Michael Moore, who are filled with such rage and hate that it's impossible to even have one brief, passing moment of appreciation for anything they've done. He has emerged as one of the most abrasive, obnoxious members of the liberal elite who use propaganda and deceit to paint conservative Republicans as evil.

Michael Moore's "documentary," *Fahrenheit 9/11,* epitomizes that senseless anger. I'll never forget sitting in the middle of a packed movie theater in Times Square in New York City watching his propaganda-filled rant. It was one of those surreal, almost out-of-body experiences. Not only did I have to sit through this awful, hate-filled movie, produced with the sole intent of defeating George Bush, but the theater was jammed with Michael Moore–loving liberals who were positively giddy over the experience.

Surrounded by idiots.

People have asked why I'd put one dime into the ample pockets of the ample renegade "documentarian." Well, I didn't pay for my movie ticket. A colleague managed to grab a free pass for the theater. Unless Moore gets a cut of popcorn sales, I didn't contribute anything to him.

I had to see his movie because that's my job. *Fahrenheit 9/11* would be a hot topic, widely discussed on my radio show and during my appearances on Fox News Channel. I needed to know what I would be criticizing. If you are going to take a work of popular culture to task, you had better be willing to actually see or read it. I squirm when watching someone rail against a particular TV show or movie then admit, "I don't need to see filth to know what it is." While high-minded, that response is impractical. If I'm going to attack a book, movie, article or speech, I'm going to actually know its content. And boy, did I have a feeling I'd be laying into *Fahrenheit 9/11*.

So there I was, uncomfortably shifting around in my seat watching Moore's movie while listening to the hoots, hollers and cheers of the New York City loony liberals surrounding me. I never saw a bigger selection of tie-dyed T-shirts and Birkenstock sandals in my life.

Most of *Fahrenheit 9/11* is just pabulum. For example, Moore managed to find outtakes of Bush administration officials getting their makeup applied for your usual TV appearances. It's a cheap shot to imply that they're performers in greasepaint.

One of the most talked-about scenes shows President Bush sitting in a Florida classroom after he was just told about the terror attacks of 9/11. Perhaps liberals like Michael Moore thought Bush should have run shrieking from the classroom in front of those schoolchildren, instead of sitting there for a few minutes before moving the traveling White House, and its hundreds of staff members and Secret Service agents, to a more secure location.

Another cheap shot.

The most egregious part of the entire movie was the way Michael Moore portrayed the American soldier. We all know that tens of thousands of soldiers have committed themselves to the war on terror. I hear their stories on my radio show every day. Noble and courageous husbands and wives, sons and daughters, brothers and sisters, men and women who are proud to do the right thing, fight for America and help spread freedom and democracy all over the world.

Moore undoubtedly had hundreds of hours of footage from his interviews with soldiers. Yet, he only chose scenes that showed them at their worst. Like the young soldier who bragged about going into battle while listening to violent lyrics like "Let the Bodies Hit the Floor," and the laughing soldiers who were taunting a wounded Iraqi and kidding about "Ali Baba." Moore used a few bad apples to make the whole bunch look like an army of crude, bloodthirsty killers who were in Iraq for the wrong reasons. Contemptible trick. Contemptible filmmaker. And positively unforgivable.

Moore attended the Democratic Convention in Boston where, naturally, he was treated like a huge star. He didn't get quite the same reception when he showed up at the Republican Convention in New York City. And his feelings about Republicans were clearly on display in a simple classless gesture.

When Senator John McCain in his convention speech made a passing reference to Moore and his movie, the sloppy "documentarian," sitting up in the cheap seats, reacted by making the "L" sign with his thumb and forefinger. Not everyone realized what most American teenagers know: *L* stands for loser.

To see that smirking giggling slob call John McCain a loser was infuriating. McCain is a true American war hero, a patriot who was tortured and held for years at a Vietnamese prison camp. Try to picture Michael Moore being subjected to the same conditions. He probably would have folded like a cheap lawn chair. Aside from distorting the truth, what exactly has Moore accomplished? Nothing, really. Except that he is so off base, he's spinning in the outer galaxies of liberal lunacy.

So it should come as no surprise that when I was presented with the opportunity to take on the master propagandist, I seized it. It was just a few weeks before the November 2004 election when Moore had emerged as a liberal guru, an anti-Bush voice who tirelessly worked to defeat the president. He toured America's college campuses, urging students to vote for Senator John Kerry. He called it his "Slacker Tour," appealing to young, impressionable college kids.

One day on the radio show, I took a call from the angry mother of a Penn State student. "Mike, can anyone explain why my daughter's university is giving $30,000 to Michael Moore so that he can come to campus and denigrate President Bush and attack our troops?"

That question grabbed my attention. "Thirty thousand dollars to that traitor?" I asked. "Hasn't he made enough money off his stupid movies, books and DVDs?"

Evidently not. His "Slacker Tour" drew thousands of college kids all over the country. It is outrageous that $30,000 in Penn State student-activity money paid for Moore's speaking fee, travel and meal expenses (in case you hadn't noticed, Moore eats a lot of meals). I knew in my heart that his presence on the campus of Penn State University must be challenged and protested. By me.

As luck would have it, one of the first stations to carry my national radio show was WRSC-AM in State College, Pennsylvania, the home of Penn State University. To protest Michael Moore's appearance there, I announced plans to take my radio show to State College on the same day. I planned to present a movie called *Fahren-HYPE 9/11,* an exposé of the lies and propaganda that Moore spewed in his ugly movie.

*Fahren-HYPE 9/11* would be staged like a good old-fashioned Hollywood premiere, complete with red carpet and velvet ropes. Besides tweaking Moore, our major objective would be raising money for our troops. (A particular passion of mine, which you'll find more about later.) My stated goal: to raise one penny more than the $30,000 that he would pocket for his Penn State appearance.

My radio audience reacted with enthusiasm. Within three days, we hit $30,000 in credit card donations through my Web site, Mikeonline.com. Money continued to pour in even after we made our goal. It was unbelievably satisfying to be able to help our troops while Moore lined his pockets urging college kids to "sleep late, drink beer, and vote for John Kerry." We would show a movie exposing Moore as a fraud while raising tens of thousands of dollars not for our pockets but for soldiers overseas.

October 22, 2004: the big day. A Penn State student group, "Young Americans for Freedom," sponsored our visit and booked the 750-seat Thomas Auditorium for our premiere. A media circus followed us around State College and Penn State. Hundreds of supporters came to the broadcast of our radio show in the lobby of the Holiday Inn Express in State College. In the crowd, a Michael Moore look-alike invited me to vent our frustrations with the *Fahrenheit 9/11* lies by hitting him in the face with a pie. Boy, did that feel good.

Then, it was on to the campus premiere of *Fahren-HYPE 9/11*. We added another movie to the lineup, a fantastic documentary called *Stolen Honor: Wounds that Never Heal.* Produced by Pulitzer Prize winner Carlton Sherwood, also a Vietnam War veteran, this movie features former Vietnam War prisoners of war blasting John Kerry. They claim their captors retaliated against them when Kerry testified in 1971 that American soldiers were guilty of war atrocities.

I'll let Nichole Dobo, of the *Centre Daily Times,* tell the rest of the story.

Deafening applause and shouts of "four more years" greeted Mike Gallagher as he walked into the Thomas Building at Penn State on Friday evening.

He briefly left the auditorium as flags, prayers and patriotic music filled the hall and photos showing images of Sept. 11, 2001, were shown. Then, the talk-show host re-entered the room, shortly after 9 p.m.

"I'm gonna start weeping," Gallagher said to more than 750 people in the audience. "I can't believe the feeling in this room tonight."

Gallagher said he was "humbled" by the huge crowd and its energy. . . .

Although Gallagher opposed spending student money to pay for an appearance by filmmaker Michael Moore at the Bryce Jordan Center, free speech at the university is important, he said.

"We know he's wrong," Gallagher said, "and we want our side to be heard, too."

Gallagher, since announcing he would come to Penn State, has been asking for contributions to send care packages to troops overseas. He said he'd raised $62,200, about 95 percent of which came from the State College area.

He had invited . . . soldiers to speak beside him.

Staff Sgt. Larry Gill, a career military officer and the recipient of two Purple Hearts—one for wounds received while serving in Iraq—said the packages will mean a lot to the soldiers in Iraq.

"It's great getting a package from home," he said. "Little things, like a bag of M&Ms that you might take for granted, really brighten our day."

Gill urged the crowd to vote for President Bush on Nov. 2.

Dave and Mary Lu Sittler, of Spring Mills, sat in the lobby for lack of any available seats in the auditorium. They donated money to Gallagher's cause, they said, to support the troops and show their displeasure for the Moore event.

"We are both Penn State alumni, and we were not pleased that student money went to fund that event," Dave Sittler said.

The night snowballed into a huge success. As Ms. Dobo noted above, we exceeded our goal of one penny more than Michael Moore's $30,000 speaking fee by more than $32,000, taking in a total of $62,000. We were able to host an event that inspired and up-lifted people on the eve of a crucial presidential election.

For the enthusiastic members of the audience who were crammed into the Thomas Building, the first moment of many that brought them to their feet came when our injured soldiers—Sergeants Larry Gill and Chris Bain—were introduced. These he-roes, being treated at Walter Reed Army Medical Center at the time for their injuries in Iraq, were with us because they supported our cause and were really irritated with Michael Moore's movie.

"I'd probably crawl over hot coals to take on the guy who made *Fahrenheit 9/11*," Sergeant Gill told me with a big grin. "If no one challenges his lies, he gets away with it."

That was the whole point. We managed to show Penn State students that it isn't just the loons like Michael Moore who get to be heard, even on a college campus. Conservatives get their plat-forms, too.

At the end of the night as we were in the airport waiting to leave, I heard a story about how shoddily Michael Moore behaves. A local police officer shook my hand and said, "Mr. Gallagher, I have to tell you something. I'm not political. I don't pay much attention to your side or Michael Moore's. But I've been with both of you guys at various times today and there's a world of difference between you two.

"Moore is a nasty, ugly man who has treated everyone around him terribly. He said some hateful things to people around him and treats everyone like dirt. You, on the other hand, have been kind and gracious to the police and everyone else. And I just wanted to say thank you for that."

His comments capped the evening and made me realize how proud I am to belong to the loyal opposition to liberals everywhere.

Another liberal I ran up against was Robert C. Byrd Jr., the senior Democratic senator from West Virginia. I'd been griping about him for years, so when I had the opportunity to meet him at the 2004 Democratic National Convention, I couldn't pass it up.

I've been attending political conventions since 1992. Radio big-mouths like me are held captive behind card tables on "radio row." Thousands of phone and cable lines, computers and microphones surround us. We yammer away simultaneously. Acoustically, it's a nightmare. Logistically, it's convenient because political operatives bring around their big-name guests, sparing us the trouble of chasing them down.

The settings for the Republican and Democratic conventions were as different as concerts by punk rocker Courtney Love and pop sweetheart Jessica Simpson. President Bush had to cope with raw Manhattan, hostile territory, a bastion of liberalism. John Kerry basked in the glow of his hometown. He was only blocks away from his Beacon Hill townhouse.

As luck would have it, my crew and I wound up staying in Beacon Hill, too. Because of the shortage of hotel rooms, we rented a nineteenth-century brick townhouse, once a stop on the Underground Railroad. The people who rented out their home to us were a delightful couple named Mary and John who also happened to be fans of the radio show.

By staying in Beacon Hill, we heard some juicy stories about John Kerry. Mary told me about the time Kerry stormed down one of the neighborhood's narrow sidewalks, stepped on her Labrador, Annie, and said, "Get that damn dog out of my way." Annie was a sweetheart of a dog. The other neighbors told me they liked Annie so much, they mourned her death at age eighteen in 1999 by erecting an impromptu sidewalk memorial, decorated with flowers, candles and cards. For three days, people kept lighting candles and adding to the display, which filled Mary's entire staircase.

Other neighbors described how Kerry routinely barged into the local coffee shop and cut in front of people standing in line. "I have a plane to catch," or, "I'm late for an appointment," he'd announce, as if that excused his rudeness. Real swell guy, eh?

So I'm living in style, strolling from Beacon Hill each morning to the Fleet Center. Once inside the convention, I felt like Van Helsing, the vampire killer, imprisoned in Castle Dracula. They did bring me some vampires, I mean Democrats, especially ones who were trying to promote their latest books, like Senator Robert Byrd. He's an old-school Democrat who has said some of the most hateful and outrageous things about the Republican Party and President Bush over the years. In his latest rant, he blamed President Bush for creating "America the bully" and disregarding the Constitution.

"The Constitution of the United States has been undercut, undermined and is under attack," Byrd said during a speech at the University of Charleston in September 2004. "I have viewed with increasing alarm the erosion of the people's liberties. What we've seen is a ruthless grab for power. This administration relies on fear and secrecy."

This from a man who once belonged to the Ku Klux Klan, the epitome of fear-mongering. Secrecy? Those guys hide behind white sheets. Given Byrd's past, it's audacious for him to rip into *anyone*. Yet the senior senator from West Virginia relishes his Republican-bashing.

So here now was Senator Byrd, eager to plug his new book, *Losing America: Confronting a Reckless and Arrogant Presidency*, and probably lob some choice barbs at President Bush. My mind raced with mischievous ideas and I invited my audience to contribute.

"I'm going to have a chance to finally confront Senator Robert Byrd," I announced. "In five minutes, he's going to be sitting here at my broadcast booth. What can we do to let this doddering, liberal lunatic know what we think of him?"

Always up for my latest hare-brained schemes, my listeners began jamming the phone lines. A young man from Columbia, South Carolina, offered the best idea. "Mike, you can't do anything directly to him or he's just going to get up and leave," said Tim, the caller. "Let me be on hold and I'll act like a supportive caller. I'll tell him how much I admire and respect him. And then, since he's a former Klansman, I'll ask him for advice on the best way to keep white sheets *really* white."

"Perfect!" I screamed. "Just perfect. Don't go anywhere; I'll put you on hold. When the time is right, I'll put you on the air and you can do your thing." Tim said he would wait for as long as it took.

About twenty minutes after we hatched our plan, down the hall tottered Senator Robert Byrd. Instead of a blustery, angry, fired-up senior citizen, Senator Byrd appeared looking quite frail and tired. He leaned heavily on a cane. His hands trembled. When he finally managed to settle into the guest chair, he said, "How wonderful to meet you, Mr. Gallagher. It is *such* an honor and pleasure to be on your radio show."

My mischief shamed me. As I began to interview the senator, there was Tim, blinking away on line seven, ready to deliver the knockout punch. The idea suddenly mortified me. Could I really humiliate this feeble, eighty-seven-year-old man?

Despite the senator's liberal lunacy, I just couldn't bring myself to mock him. I ended the five-minute interview, watched Byrd amble precariously away and never launched Tim. To reward the caller for his patience, I sent him a great prize reserved for special listeners, a cheesecake from the Carnegie Deli in New York, a *Gallagher Show* favorite. Tim was pleased.

I felt good that I didn't lower myself to the shock tactics of ideologues like Michael Moore. It's unlikely that Moore would have shown such restraint.

Later that night, back in our headquarters on Beacon Hill, I told Denise the whole story. Her eyes widened with horror as I talked about the caller who was ready to ask Byrd about his Klan background. But when I told her how I just couldn't pull a stunt like that on a little old man who was clearly nearing the end of life's journey, she said she was proud of me.

"You did good, Gallagher," she said. "You know, for a big blow-hard Republican, you're not half bad." And she gave me a big kiss.

You know, for a Democrat, she's not too bad, either.

The liberal agenda permeates everything we see and hear. When not taking on activist politicians, we have to do battle with the leftist voices on the airwaves. Fortunately, I get a chance to do that regularly on Fox News Channel.

The setting is like my second home: the Fox News Channel affiliate in Dallas. It's Monday, July 2, 2003, and I'm appearing on Fox's highly rated *Hannity and Colmes.* I'm scheduled to debate Ellen Ratner, White House correspondent and bureau chief for the Talk Radio News service and a Fox News analyst. A pleasant woman off-camera, she transforms into a shrill mouthpiece for the Democrats when the red light comes on. She's one of my frequent sparring partners on Fox.

The lefties love to smear Fox News Channel as a conservative front. As usual, they just don't get it. Fox appeals to viewers across the political landscape. The network's soaring ratings confound media elitists who worship at the altars of National Public Radio and the *New York Times.* They wonder how this all-news cable operation attracts so many people, why the public is abuzz over Bill O'Reilly's *Factor,* Shepherd Smith's hip appeal or the latest dust-up between conservative Sean Hannity and liberal Alan Colmes.

There's a simple answer. Fox News Channel's chief architect, Roger Ailes, designed a format that offers fair and balanced coverage of news and issues. Combine that formula with savvy broadcasters, eye-catching graphics and the balance of hard news and light features, and just like that baseball field in an Iowa cornfield, people will come.

In my many appearances on Fox News Channel, almost every time I appear the network also invites someone considered my ideological opposite. Fox pairs a liberal commentator with just about every conservative guest. Ailes didn't create a one-sided network. He just believes that conservatives deserve a fair hearing, which the mainstream media often denies them.

So, that night in the Dallas bureau I was primed for yet another showdown with a liberal. We were dissecting a new Gallup poll that found 80 percent of conservatives are proud of America. However, 68 percent of moderates and only 56 percent of liberals agreed. To me, that meant that Republicans were, by extension, more patriotic than Democrats. Alan and Ellen disagreed.

"This Gallup poll confirms what we've known forever, Sean," I said. "And that is, of course, conservatives are more patriotic than liberals. Liberal Democrats are un-American and they have been since the Iraqi war began."

"Ellen?" Sean asked.

"I think Samuel Johnson said that patriotism was the last refuge of scoundrels," she said. "I mean, really, it does not take into account that many Americans who may not be proud of what the United States did at this point in time, would fight and die for our rights, our rights to be free, our rights to say things. It's a very different question."

As the conversation continued, I suddenly had a burst of inspiration. Often my best lines come to me only after my TV appearances, usually while driving home. Not this time.

"Are *you* proud to be an American?" I asked Ellen.

"I would say I'm very glad to be an American," she said. "I'm not proud of what the United States is doing right now in Iraq. That's what I would say."

"You're amazing," I said. "So in other words, you can't even say yes to the question 'are you proud to be an American?' "

Alan, trying to overcompensate, no doubt, jumped in to say he was very proud to be an American. Not Ellen.

"Like Alan," she said, "I'm proud to be in America, and I would fight and die for our rights. And that's very different."

"Ellen, you ought to be ashamed," Sean said a few moments later. "Ellen Ratner, you're not proud to be an American? I didn't even think to ask you that question."

"There are soldiers who I am proud of," she answered. "And I'm proud of the job they are doing in Iraq. But I am not proud of the fact that we went into Iraq and invaded Iraq. There's a very different issue. Am I glad to be an American? Absolutely. Would I die for our rights in this country? Absolutely."

"Ask every liberal Democrat you want," I shot back, "and that's the kind of answer you'll get, Sean and Alan. It's about 50 percent at best. Shame on you, Ellen."

Hundreds of Americans e-mailed me, outraged that Ellen Ratner, a liberal talking head, could not say "Yes, I'm proud to be an American" on national television.

> Mike, how can you stand to even talk to that woman on TV? I cannot believe what I just saw. She actually refused to admit that she was proud to be an American. She's a typical liberal nitwit and you nailed her. Way go to!
>
> Kevin

Ellen Ratner is the poster girl for liberalism in America today. Your brilliant method of holding her feet to the fire made my husband and I scream for joy as we were watching you on Fox, Mike. Congratulations on proving the point that liberals hate America.

Janice and Frank

Hooray for being able to get a liberal to admit what we've been suspecting all along, Gallagher—that liberals refuse to even admit to being proud Americans. I wish Ellen would pack her bags and move to Afghanistan or someplace where maybe she can see what it's like over there. She can take Barbra Streisand, et al. with her!!

W.L.

Not everybody sent me a complimentary e-mail, though:

How dare you attack Ellen or Alan's patriotism, you big, fat bag of wind? You right wing Nazis think that if you put a flag on your lapel and blindly follow W. into the battlefield, you're more patriotic than those of us progressives. You conservative zealots make me want to puke.

Barry

Well, I hope you're feeling better, Mr. "Progressive." Try some Pepto-Bismol. Better still, recite the pledge of allegiance. You'll feel better.

I understand that Ellen Ratner is just one individual who might not be considered the official spokesperson for liberalism in America.

Then again, no one person is. However, I believe Ellen to be a sincere follower of the liberal agenda that has poisoned our nation.

Conservatives don't have to qualify something as simple as expressing pride in being an American. Practically from the day we entered our first classroom and put our hand over our heart and pledged allegiance, under God, to the United States of America, we loved our country. We believe in it. And we understand the sacrifice our founding fathers and those who have fought for us have made in securing a nation that we can love with all our hearts.

Liberals like Ellen Ratner seem to gravitate toward the things that they think are wrong with America. It's as if they're uncomfortable with an expression of patriotism or support for the red, white and blue. Their antimilitary, anticapitalism, antigovernment rhetoric makes them sound like proponents of a banana republic dictatorship, rather than a freedom-loving people who appreciate democracy.

The polling data so hotly debated that night on *Hannity and Colmes* was right: liberals are not only unpatriotic, they don't even like America.

# 2

# GALLAGHER'S ARMY

A Colorado teacher was the last straw.

In the winter of 2003, Martha Swisher was teaching at West Jefferson Middle School in Conifer, a mountain town west of Denver. A Denver listener's e-mail raged about her.

> Mike, you're not going to believe this: there's a teacher who started wearing a button on her coat to a school field trip that said, "HE'S NOT MY PRESIDENT." The kids are confused and wondering why Miss Swisher hates the president.
>
> Not only is the school district not firing this manipulative woman, they're actually *defending* her! The teacher's union says it's a matter of free speech. Mike, do something about this!

It was signed "Damned Mad in Denver."

It made me damned mad, too. Imagine the gall of that teacher, flaunting her contempt for our president to her students. And this was during wartime. If she wants, wear that button to a flag burning—not on a school trip. It was another example of the liberal idiocy that is poisoning our classrooms.

It seems like every week, I hear from a concerned parent about the latest act of insanity from a liberal teacher in a public classroom. One outraged parent called me from California to complain about a teacher who favored giving condoms to a health class for fourteen- and fifteen-year-olds. Another worried mom wanted to know if she had any recourse against a teacher who refused to allow her daughter to wear a small cross on a chain around her neck.

These outrages are happening in communities all over America. Take it from me; it's not just in New York or Los Angeles or Chicago. I hear about these teacher shenanigans from parents in cities like Greenville, South Carolina, and Decatur, Illinois, and South Bend, Indiana.

With the Colorado incident, some parents decided to fight back. They'd had enough of ideologically driven teachers' influence over our children for years, without anybody being able to stop them. Linda Fowler, whose thirteen-year-old son Andrew was in Swisher's class, decided to lead an effort to ban school employees from wearing political buttons in front of the kids.

"Both my husband and I were very offended by it. My son, who's in the sixth grade, had some very confused feelings, very hurtful feelings about the whole thing," she told the *Rocky Mountain News.*

At first, the school's principal said the teacher was protected under the First Amendment. Eventually, though, the school district ruled that Martha Swisher and other teachers had to remove political buttons while at work. Republicans at the Colorado statehouse honored the Fowler family for their stand.

My radio show follows a simple format. Each hour, I begin with a news item or great talk topic. I give my opinions, and then invite listeners to air theirs. During commercials, I read and answer e-mails, pore over the newspapers, make appointments, think of future topics, line up guests or even call my wife. I dash to make progress during those four-and-a-half-minute breaks. For me, this system works, allows me to plan, think ahead and sometimes come up with surprises.

The day of the Colorado teacher story, my anger simmering during one of the commercial breaks, I was inspired. I didn't realize it at first, but Gallagher's Army was being born.

I remembered hearing about a charity from Oklahoma City, Feed the Children. Founder Larry Jones and his team were bringing truckloads of food and personal-care items to families with relatives in the military, people whose loved ones were fighting for our freedom.

The company that syndicates my show, Salem Radio Network, had worked with Feed the Children for years. So on my first commercial break that day, I called Larry Jones. I'm sure he thought I was nuts.

ME: Larry, it's Mike Gallagher. How much does it cost to fill up one of your semi tractor-trailers with items for military families?

ERIC HANSEN *(my engineer and ever-present voice in my head-phones):* Coming back in one minute, Mike.

LARRY: Well Mike, it takes a lot of giving and generosity and well-meaning people who want to . . .

ME: No, no, I mean how much does it *cost?* What's the dollar value of the items you deliver?

LARRY: Are we on the air? Because I'm happy to tell you what each box of food and personal-care items cost, but I'm not sure where you're going with this . . .

ERIC: Thirty seconds, Mike.

ME: Larry, I know I sound crazy, but I just want to raise enough money for one truckload for military families. What does it cost?

LARRY: Well, the boxes contain shaving cream, boxes of maca-roni and cheese, even skin lotion, things that struggling families might not even . . .

ERIC: Ten seconds to air, Mike.

ME: Larry, I get it, I really do, but I need to know, *what does one truck cost?*

LARRY: Approximately $7,000. That provides about 550 boxes and we like to give two boxes to each family.

ME: Perfect, Larry. That's what I needed to know. I'll call you after the show.

PETER RIEF (*staff announcer*): . . . and now back to the *Mike Gallagher Show!*

Okay, so it costs $7,000 to fill up a truck and deliver it to a bunch of military families. What if I could get my listeners, who were as furious as I was about this teacher, to donate $7,000 bucks? What if we could take a negative and turn it into a giant positive? Maybe we could channel our anger and frustration into goodwill and bring a truckload of food and personal-care items to Colorado military families. Heck, I could even sit up in the cab of the truck and blow the horn as we drove by the school where Miss What's-Her-Name pulled her stunt!

On the air again, I spoke carefully. I had never raised money on my show before. I wasn't even sure if my boss, Greg Anderson, would approve. After all, it's a radio show, not a telethon. But the gesture felt right. If trouble followed, so be it. Better to beg forgiveness than ask for permission, an approach that has served me well over the years.

"You know, I've been thinking about it—a lot—and I have a crazy idea," I told my listeners. "I'm not sure if it's going to work, but hear me out. What if we took this awful story about the teacher in Colorado and turned it into something positive? I'm hoping we can raise $7,000 today and be able to take a truckload of gifts to military families."

I told the audience about my conversation with Larry Jones and exactly what $7,000 would mean.

"If you agree with me about the need to help our military families and remind them that they're not alone right now, that we support and honor them, then put your money where your mouth is and help me. My wife and I will start with a $1,000 donation. So all we need is $6,000. Let's do it!"

Then I announced a special toll free number, which we managed to set up on short notice, and hoped (and prayed) that the phones would ring.

Two hours later, the phones still rang. They rang all day. We didn't raise $7,000. By day's end, the pledges topped $90,000.

Instead of one truck, we would be sending at least thirteen. And if one truck would bring comfort to 225 military families, then our quick fund-raiser would help almost 3,000. My smile lasted for days. My wife said I was as close to giddy as she'd ever seen me. For the first time in my career, I felt that my show really mattered to people.

I had always known we had connected with the public. In trips across the country, people were constantly shaking my hand, asking about my kids, or commiserating over left-wing nonsense. This time, I knew our show galvanized people into action. My listeners helped thousands of military families who were having a tough time paying the electric bill. That is as good as it gets.

When I saw that my radio show could actually be a catalyst, I wanted to expand the fund-raising. Why stop in Colorado? Families all over the country could use our help. We soon created a slogan: Gallagher's Army.

Everytime I'd appeal for money, listeners heard a bugle. "Okay, troops, this is your general speaking," I'd bellow. "It's time to rally the troops. We need to let these military families know that we're thinking of them as their loved ones fight for our country."

It worked. We kept raising money for brave families in San Diego, California, Fayetteville, North Carolina, Phoenix, Arizona, and Colorado. Larry Jones and I traveled to these places, handing out gift boxes to military families. It wasn't charity as much as a little dose of goodness from all of us who wanted those families to know how much we appreciated their service to America.

I had always believed that a successful radio show featured a basic formula: entertain, inform, be provocative, deliver solid ratings and healthy revenues. But suddenly, I realized that a national radio show could be much more. We could put the show to good use and actually create a fund-raising vehicle, a way to help deserving people. Why not do great radio *and* good things for people? And what's a better cause than the brave soldiers who are serving our country, and their supportive families?

Shortly after this project got started, Denise and I were out to dinner with some friends of ours and excitedly talking about what was happening with Gallagher's Army. We embarked upon an ambitious plan: let's make it official. One of those friends, Joey Hudson, became the director of Gallagher's Army—the Mike Gallagher Show Charitable Foundation, which formalized our vision.

Creating the foundation and raising money for our troops and their families have been so uplifting. I'm more proud of our work here than of any other achievement in my twenty-seven-year career. Since 2002, with the support of the Salem Radio Network, we've raised nearly two millions dollars for the cause. That's a lot of big-hearted *Mike Gallagher Show* listeners pledging and sending five, ten, twenty, one hundred dollars. Thank you all.

While immensely rewarding, the foundation and on-air fund-raising have brought plenty of distractions, headaches and worries. Do we have the right amount of liability insurance? How much is too much for our expenses? Should an issues-oriented radio talk show be a format for raising money?

Only one radio station program director objected. He was both station manager and on-air talent, a common dual role for a small market station like his in Eau Claire, Wisconsin.

I had been on this particular station for about three years and had done quite well for them. Yet when this guy, a self-described liberal, came to town, he didn't like anything about me. Hated my politics, my on-air style, and most of all, it seemed, he didn't like us raising money for the troops. "Gallagher's show sounds like a Jerry Lewis telethon," he'd complain. "He's just a right-winger who shills for Bush and the neocons and I hate how he keeps asking for money."

His criticism stung. I had always worried about that kind of reaction to Gallagher's Army. And even though this guy was a liberal who just disliked my show, I have always tried to keep every affiliate happy, even ones in small markets. In national radio, a host doesn't have one boss, we have one at every station—in my case, over two hundred. It's hard to please all of them.

Eventually, we decided to move to another radio station in Eau Claire. Yes, it was smaller but they appreciated our work. It's good to go where you're wanted.

Whenever I'd get worried about a guy like him, I'd think about how it feels to meet the parents of soldiers who are fighting this difficult war. I've met hundreds of them, mothers and fathers who have thanked me for Gallagher's Army. Often with tears in their eyes, many of them say it means so much to know that at least my listeners remember, honor and support their son's or daughter's sacrifice and dedication.

Feedback like that from one single parent of an American soldier allows me to completely disregard a pinhead like the grumpy liberal host from Eau Claire, Wisconsin.

I've been blessed to visit with wounded soldiers injured on the battlegrounds of the war on terror, guys like Sergeant Larry Gill from Semmes, Alabama, and Staff Sergeant Chris Bain from Williamsport, Pennsylvania. These Purple Heart recipients have traveled with me to Gallagher's Army events around the country, including the State College *Faren-HYPE 9/11* screening I wrote about earlier. They help spread the word about the good America has achieved in Iraq and Afghanistan.

Both of these brave heroes were badly injured in Iraq and spent months at the Walter Reed Army Medical Center in Washington, D.C.

"I've gone from wheelchair to walker to crutches to cane and now the leg brace," said Sergeant Gill, forty-five, of the Army National Guard. A hand grenade lobbed by Iraqi insurgents on a Baghdad highway blew open Sergeant Gill's legs on October 7, 2003. He lost more than nine inches from his left calf muscle, nerves and arteries in his lower left leg. It's taken six surgeries and a year of physical therapy for him to limp along with a brace on his useless left foot.

Ambushed in a mortar attack, Sergeant Bain ran for cover only after making sure other soldiers were safe. He and his men had been inside an Army base north of Baghdad on April 8, 2004, when Iraqis in a foxhole just outside the security perimeter opened fire.

"I was a master fitness instructor, now I can't even do a push-up," said Sergeant Bain, thirty-four, an Army Reservist. Shrapnel ripped open Sergeant Bain's left forearm, obliterating muscle and tendons. On his left hand, the blast severed his ring finger and blew off the tip of his pinky. Nerve damage from being shot in his right elbow has deadened half of his right hand. Eight operations and months of physical therapy later, Sergeant Bain has learned again how to write, drive and get dressed.

Both men cope with physical pain and anxiety every day. Sergeant Bain suffers from flashbacks. Sergeant Gill worries about how he'll support his family in the future. Despite their injuries and long rehabilitation, both soldiers believe in the war on terror.

"We've been called everything from occupiers on down," said Sergeant Gill. "You can look at my torn-up legs and realize there are people who don't like us over there. But the majority of people we dealt with in Iraq were glad to see us, welcomed our help and needed our assistance."

"I would do it again, in a heartbeat," said Sergeant Bain. "I think we're doing great things over there. For me, I'd go through pain everyday as long as we're doing what we're doing. Let's not leave until we get the job done in Iraq and Afghanistan."

Their resolve remains strong, their spirits high. They understand what's at stake and gladly continue to support the United States of America. Chris Bain and Larry Gill will both tell you that they are the kinds of soldiers who best represent those on the field of battle, not the handful of malcontents in Michael Moore's propaganda-drenched movie.

My Web site, Mikeonline.com, has become a crucial tool in collecting funds for the troops. We're real proud of the way our Web site has evolved. Like most effective radio show Web sites, we offer streaming audio, behind-the-scenes photos, biographies, links to opinion pieces and other goodies. We also always reserve a place on our Web site where people can pledge donations for the brave men and women who are risking their lives for the greatest country in the world.

Gallagher's Army has led me to form a number of special relationships with soldiers and their families, and, just as important, an ability to see this war on terror through their eyes, from their perspective.

Over and over again, they tell me how crucial it was for our country to launch a pre-emptive strike against Iraq and topple Saddam Hussein, a madman who was plenty willing and able to assist terrorists who want to kill more innocent American civilians. They remind me that in the months after 9/11, Americans expected President Bush to uphold his promise to take the war on terror to any corner of the globe that poses a threat to the safety and security of the United States.

They've also expressed disgust with the loony liberals who pretend to support the troops while condemning the war on terror and the administration. These soldiers, their moms and dads, their family and friends, repeatedly point out the absurdity of liberals trying to have it both ways: claiming to support the soldier but attacking his efforts.

One proud military dad I met had a great analogy that perfectly exposes the flaw in the liberal's logic. "It's like saying you love all the individual players on the Dallas Cowboys, but you hate the coach so you hope they lose all of their games. Sorry, kids, it doesn't work that way. You either root for the team to win or you don't."

Let's all face the grim reality that the world is filled with evil, cowardly terrorists who want to slaughter innocent men, women and children, only because we're Americans. The wars in Afghanistan and Iraq have been the opening volleys. We're going to have to accept the fact that we'll be fighting a war on terror for the rest of our lives, maybe our children's and grandchildren's lives, too.

So let's understand this war's nature, accept the challenges, and wholeheartedly support our president and the men and women who are on the front lines fighting it. We need to reject the message of people like Michael Moore, and all the other left-leaning voices who want to root against our team.

As President Bush said, you're either with us or with the terrorists.

After six months, we started to run out of hooks for the fundraising. Donations stalled. I've always understood the old saying about good things having to come to an end. But I just didn't want to see the end of our efforts on behalf of the military families. For a few weeks, I was depressed, anxious and worried about the future of our plans to continue raising money for the soldiers. I figured the end was near. Then Natalie Maines, lead singer of the Dixie Chicks country band, opened her big mouth and a second wind lifted us along.

# 3

# MIKE VERSUS THE SADDAM CHICKS

*Oh but I was just young, I was scared, I was wrong*

—"A HOME" BY THE DIXIE CHICKS

I was indifferent to the Dixie Chicks, the chart-topping country music trio from Texas. My musical tastes range from crooner Harry Connick Jr. to pop rocker Harry Nilsson to jazz phenomenon Norah Jones. But I knew enough about the Dixie Chicks to have recognized how big they were in 2003. Real big. It was the year of their runaway hit single, appropriately named "Landslide," first made famous by Stevie Nicks and Fleetwood Mac. The Dixie Chicks's multiplatinum album *Home* earned the sexy trio four Grammy Awards, bringing their total to seven.

Anyway, I didn't like or dislike them. That changed, though, on

Monday, March 10, 2003. From a London stage that evening, Dixie Chicks lead singer Natalie Maines crossed the line from peace activism into nastiness and bad taste.

"Just so you know," she told the British audience, "we are ashamed that the president of the United States is from Texas. We do not want war."

I immediately denounced her comments on my radio show. It was bad enough that some ditzy singer expressed her antiwar feelings in an inappropriate personal attack on our president. But blasting our leader like this during wartime to the British, our steadfast allies? Unforgivable.

It was also maddening to realize that she didn't seem to have enough nerve to blast our president on American soil; she had to pop off at a concert overseas. Maybe she thought her diatribe wouldn't make its way back to the United States. If so, boy, was she ever mistaken.

My protest joined a chorus of outraged Americans. Folks in Nashville, Dallas and San Diego jammed radio station phone lines, urging a boycott of Dixie Chicks songs.

In a resolution, the South Carolina House of Representatives demanded an apology specifically to their state and a free Dixie Chicks concert for the troops. Ex-fans in Louisiana drove a tractor over a pile of the group's CDs. Country music singer Travis Tritt scolded Maines:

"When you [say] we're ashamed our president comes from the same state we do, it comes off as being cowardly because it was done across the ocean. I dare her to go to the Astrodome and say that. Also, it's a cheap shot against one individual."

Performer Toby Keith, whose songs support a tough military response to terrorism, flashed a photoshopped picture of Maines with Saddam Hussein during his concerts.

Even President Bush commented on the backlash against his fellow Texans, telling NBC anchor Tom Brokaw:

"The Dixie Chicks are free to speak their mind. They can say what they want to say . . . freedom is a two-way street . . . I don't really care what the Dixie Chicks said. I want to do what I think is right for the American people. And if . . . some singers or Hollywood stars feel like speaking out, that's fine. That's the great thing about America."

I know that reporters have jobs to do and that they had to ask President Bush about this since it became such a national furor. But can you imagine what was going through the mind of the leader of the free world, expected to opine about some bigmouth, pampered, privileged singer?

I learned that the Dixie Chicks planned to kick off their Top of the World North American tour on May 1, 2003, in a place I know and love: Greenville, South Carolina. It was in Greenville where my life came together in the late '80s and early '90s. I met and fell in love with Denise in Greenville, married her there and cut my teeth in talk radio at what was then WFBC-AM. I still consider Greenville home. To this day, two of our sons and my in-laws live there.

I hatched a plan: stage a "counter" concert, an anti–Dixie Chicks event, with all of the profits going to, you guessed it, military families.

"Are you completely out of your mind?" my boss asked in a pleasant voice. Greg Anderson always has a way of being upbeat while saying flat out that he just cannot fathom my latest harebrained stunt.

"You have no idea what it takes to promote a concert," he said. "We're not staffed for this, you don't know anything about doing this, and we're not in the concert promotion business." Blah, blah, blah. I had heard it all before.

While Greg is one of the finest broadcast executives I know, not to mention a longtime friend, he's always convinced that I overextend myself. But I believed in this idea, and Greg believes in me.

So after a few days hearing me beg and plead, he finally said yes. The Gallagher's Army Benefit Concert for Military Families was a go. Now we just had to find the bands.

Quickly, I assembled a staff. Like it or not, I was, indeed, the promoter. Eric Hansen, my show's operations manager and engineer, would coordinate the technical and operational aspects. Harriet Hofmann of our network sales staff would be the liaison with Feed the Children, the event's beneficiary. Darcy Peterson, our network sales promotions director, would try and hire the bands. The four of us became "the team." It would all rest on our shoulders.

"I think people are so upset about the Dixie Chicks that if I have to get a banjo and stand up there on stage and sing 'On Top of Old Smoky' people will stand up and cheer, they don't care," I told the Associated Press. "Obviously this is designed to send a message that it's not okay to run down our president during this time of war. They insulted their core audience. Country music fans are red-blooded, patriotic Americans who support our military and support our commander in chief."

Our headliner had to be a country music band, we decided. Since the Dixie Chicks were country, we'd take them on in their own musical backyard. Darcy used her contacts in Nashville and the recording industry and contacted the Marshall Tucker Band. They quickly accepted our invitation.

Thirty years in the business and still going strong, this legendary country and southern rock group hailed from Greenville/Spartanburg, South Carolina, precisely the venue for our concert.

Since their 1972 debut, the Marshall Tucker Band has produced seven gold and three platinum albums featuring hits like "Fire on the Mountain," "Can't You See," and "Heard It in a Love Song."

Their lead singer, Doug Gray, is a Vietnam War veteran and the only founding member still with the band. He was gung-ho about fund-raising for the troops:

"We all, as Americans, should support the decision, made on behalf of our government, to insure our future and the future of our children," he said. "I support this effort and I know I am not alone in my beliefs. Support our troops and *Stand Up for America!*"

With a name band now in our corner, I began soliciting tapes and e-mails from amateur musicians. Hundreds poured in, from the Elvis impersonator in a nun's habit to proud mothers touting their nine-year-olds as the biggest talents since Patsy Cline. We waded through a mountain of tapes, CDs, letters, faxes and even Polaroid pictures of people who wanted to participate in our big night.

We eventually settled on a group called SHILOH. These five young men performed one of the most stirring renditions of the National Anthem I had ever heard. They have a great sound and I'm convinced they're going to be huge stars one day soon.

We also picked a fifteen-year-old rising singer from San Diego, a kid named Ty Nelson. Ty is the oldest of triplets. Singing in churches and other venues since the age of six, he has performed in London and is a young man with a big voice and a country swagger.

Now the lineup was complete. We had an entire evening's worth of wonderful musicians. I'd be the master of ceremonies. My old friend Russ Cassell, the legendary local morning host on WORD-AM, our affiliate in Greenville/Spartanburg, would be my onstage cohost. The Spartanburg Memorial Auditorium was booked. Anyone who had bought Dixie Chicks tickets but came to our concert instead would be ushered to a VIP section and invited to a special reception.

In a broadcasting career that spanned twenty-seven years, one of my best times was that hectic week leading up to the May 1 concert. TV crews were waiting for me when my plane landed at the Greenville/Spartanburg Airport a few days before the event. It was even more of a circus because of the new security team shadowing me, hired after some ridiculous anonymous nuts sent in threats against me.

The most prominent threat seemed to be a series of e-mails we received from some goofy group that wanted to get close enough to douse me with bright red paint. It appears they wanted to show the world that I was dripping with the blood of the Iraqis killed by Americans.

I began thinking about which of my suits I could afford to have ruined.

All of us in the public arena unfortunately have to deal with threats and stalkers at some point, especially those of us who get paid to express strong opinions about controversial issues. One time, a disturbing series of letters began arriving at the studios from a woman who was quite graphic in the way she wanted me to meet my

Maker. The police tracked her down and paid her a visit. During questioning, the officers noticed her sitting on her living room couch in a way that suggested she was hiding something. They asked if they could look under her couch, and after hesitating, she finally agreed. There, they found the typewriter that she had been using to write me, as well as a stack of newspaper articles and photos of me with huge, red slash marks across my face. One of the detectives told me it was like a scene from a bad Lifetime movie. After their little visit, I never heard from her again.

In the days leading up to the concert, in between broadcasting my regular radio shows and planning event logistics, I gave print and broadcast interviews everywhere I went. The local and national media billed it as the Anti-Dixie Chicks Concert or the Dueling Concerts in South Carolina. Splashed over front pages in the local newspapers, the event also headlined the newscasts. TV stations promoted their "team coverage" of our event. Fox News, NBC and CNN covered it. Thanks to all this attention, we managed to sell more than $100,000 worth of tickets. The Gallagher's Army Benefit Concert for Military Families was a runaway success.

Supporters of our concert blasted the Dixie Chicks in interviews with South Carolina's newspaper *The State*. Jamie Barnes, seventeen, blasted the group as "cowards. We call them Saddam Chicks," he told the paper.

I told the paper that as long as America is still threatened in the world, I would criticize the Dixie Chicks. "We still have to worry about Syria, North Korea and the terrorists," I said. "The war is not over by any means. Until all the soldiers come home, I'm afraid we're going to have to be a thorn in their side."

To me, the concert itself was a blur. I remember seeing thousands of people spring to their feet and cheer wildly when I appeared onstage, likely the first and last time that will ever happen in my lifetime. Larry Jones began the concert with an invocation (take *that*, *ACLU*). SHILOH moved us when they sang "The Star-Spangled Banner." Their repertoire of original songs also wowed the audience.

Young Ty Nelson belted out famous country hits with patriotic themes as well as some of his own tunes. And finally, the grizzled veterans of the Marshall Tucker Band put on a great show.

More stirring and important than the music was a tribute to the late Nolen Ryan Hutchings and his family. He was a nineteen-year-old Marine private from nearby Boiling Springs, South Carolina. Idolizing the Marines as a kid, he joined up soon after graduating from high school in 2000. Ryan was assigned to the 1st Battalion, 2nd Marine Regiment, 2nd Marine Expeditionary Brigade headquartered at Camp Lejeune, North Carolina.

Carolyn and Larry Hutchings had endured a year of uncertainty waiting to hear how their son died in the first days of fighting in Iraq, on March 23, 2003. The answer was heartbreaking: friendly fire. The young man's unit was trying to help secure a bridge near the city of Nasiriyah in southern Iraq. This mission was key, a vital position that could clear the way for the march to Baghdad.

However, two American fighter jets mistook the Marines for the enemy. The Air Force A-10s rained down missiles and bombs, killing at least eight Marines, including Hutchings. Officials informed Larry Hutchings that an Iraqi grenade also hit his son's vehicle, but "they don't know which hit it first," he told the *Los Angeles Times.*

At the time, Ryan was only the second soldier from South Carolina to die in Iraq. Local leaders had arranged for a state resolution honoring Hutchings and his family, which we gave them onstage during the concert. Those moments with the Hutchings family symbolized the heart and soul of our event and made the hassle and work all worthwhile.

When we presented Larry Jones with a ceremonial oversized check for $102,357 we all cried, applauded and cheered for what seemed like forever. I'll always remember that amazing week in wonderful South Carolina.

Liberals were unhappy with our efforts to shame the Dixie Chicks. I knew that would happen. But I was fascinated with the approach they took. They tried to spin the event into a free speech debate. "Don't you think you're trampling on the free speech rights of the Dixie Chicks?" asked one of the reporters who stuck a microphone in my face. "Doesn't Natalie Maines have a right to express her opinion about the president?" screeched another. I couldn't keep from laughing out loud.

"Of course they had a right to rip our president," I kept saying. "But just like you left-leaning reporters want to defend the right of Hollywood celebrities and entertainers to spout off, we should be able to defend the right of *our* side to express support for our military, our president, and our country." There really wasn't much they could say.

Liberals love to cling to the concept of free speech as an excuse to drag America through the mud. They never think the First Amendment applies to conservative points of view, too. Burn a flag, fine and dandy. Call George W. Bush a Nazi war criminal, no problem. But dare to suggest that Natalie Maines was wrong to ridicule our commander in chief in wartime and an all-out bloodbath erupts over the alleged trampling of the U.S. Constitution.

For a brief period during this patriotic week in South Carolina I thought we might manage to even influence the Dixie Chicks themselves. After arriving in South Carolina for the concert, I decided on another approach to the group. On behalf of my listeners, I offered to publicly forgive Natalie Maines and the Dixie Chicks if they would match the amount of money we raised at our concert from the profits from their opening night show at the nearby Bi-Lo Center in Greenville (five times larger than our arena, by the way). When I floated this idea on the air, many listeners objected, saying I shouldn't let the Dixie Chicks off the hook. I explained that if it meant another hundred grand for military families in one night, we shouldn't mind if the Dixie Chicks managed to save a little face.

I never thought they'd buy it. But one afternoon, my director of security for the concert, John Ratteree, ran up to me with a big grin and some exciting news. He talked to the Dixie Chicks's security chief, Lou Palumbo, who suggested that my idea might work. But the Dixie Chicks worried that my offer wasn't legitimate, that I was just trying to set them up. John promised Palumbo that I was, indeed, sincere in offering the olive branch in return for that generous contribution.

"Tell them I'll meet with them in person and show them how sincere I am," I said to John. "I'll prove it to them." John relayed the offer to Palumbo, a former New York City detective who seemed intrigued and amused by the entire situation. Sure enough, John's cell phone rang and the meeting was arranged: the Dixie Chicks invited us to their swanky digs, the Poinsett Hotel in downtown Greenville, where we would present the offer in person.

No media, no hype, just John and me. I was pumped. We were

at an event in Spartanburg, about thirty minutes away. Racing to our car, we flew down I-85.

When we arrived in Greenville within six blocks of their hotel, John's phone rang again with disappointing news. The meeting was off, there would be no deal. Palumbo simply told John that the Dixie Chicks had changed their minds.

Exasperated, I took great relish in telling my radio audience how we almost recruited the Dixie Chicks for our fund-raising efforts benefiting American military families only to have the country music divas snub us at the last minute. Imagine how much goodwill they would have enjoyed for putting aside ideological differences about our president and the war and uniting with us in a noble cause. I guess that helping military families wasn't all that important to Natalie Maines, Emily Robison and Martie Maguire.

Later that year, they announced that they were renouncing the country music industry altogether. How wonderful of them to turn their backs on an industry and millions of fans who made them rich and famous. That news made me glad I picked a fight with them in the first place.

# 4

# IF YOU CAN MAKE IT THERE, YOU'LL MAKE IT ANYWHERE . . . BUT IS IT REALLY WORTH IT?

I fell in love with talk radio as a sixteen-year-old mailroom clerk at a construction company in Dayton, Ohio.

As the only son of a working-class woman who lost her husband to leukemia when I was eleven years old, it made sense for me to work while I was going to high school. Mom was a legal secretary with bills to pay and a teenage son going to a Catholic high school with tuition due.

One of my parents' longtime friends was a kind man named Charlie Danis who ran B.G. Danis, a huge construction company in Dayton. Knowing that my mom, Marge, was a single working mother with a teenage son to raise, Mr. Danis offered to get me a job at his company. It sounded like a great gig: working in the mailroom with a guy named Grady.

Grady loved listening to talk radio. This was 1976 and there were just a few talk radio stations in America. Dayton had one: WAVI 1210AM. A feisty little station, it featured some wildly entertaining hosts. Chris Mitchell was the urbane, witty host, and the program director of the station, too. Brad Clay was a legendary radio broadcaster in Dayton, an occasionally confrontational "I'm never wrong" kind of guy. Bob Kwesell was the brash, loud-mouthed host who frequently screamed at callers, "Get off my phone, you big banana!"

It had news, drama and humor: I was hooked.

It's a miracle that any mail ever got delivered at B.G. Danis Construction because I spent as much time in the mailroom as I could, listening to every word of "People Power WAVI/Dayton." I was probably a lousy hire for B.G. Danis. But I found my career there. I began dreaming of the day when I would walk into WAVI and get a job as a talk show host.

Unbelievably, that day actually came, and it was pretty straightforward. I gave myself a little pep talk: "You have a car, Mike, figure out WAVI's address, drive over there and just tell the receptionist that you want to take a tour." Then I did it. Just like that.

The station was on Cincinnati Street right off Interstate 75, near the University of Dayton arena. As I sheepishly walked inside, I saw pictures of all my heroes lining the lobby walls. All the guys I had listened to for hours and hours smiled down on me: Brad, Bob, Art Barrett, Raymond Graham, Jim Boz and newsman Don Mills. I was thrilled.

Somehow, I managed to talk the receptionist into letting me take a look around the studios. She called program director Chris Mitchell on the intercom and he gave me a tour.

Afterward, we headed back into his office and began talking about radio. He appreciated my enthusiasm. I had seen a memo on a hallway bulletin board that said the station was looking for a fresh, young "talkmaster" (the fairly pretentious title the station used for talk host back then).

Young talkmaster? Heck, how's seventeen years old grab you, Mr. Manager? I made my pitch to Chris. "I'm your man, Mr. Mitchell. You throw me in that studio and you'll be amazed at how well I'll do," I confidently proclaimed, despite never having worked a day in radio.

Chris Mitchell looked up from some papers he was reading at his desk and suddenly said, "You know what, young man? We have a part-time host who was scheduled to go on tonight and he just called in sick. How about filling in for him?"

I was in. When I sat down in front of a real radio board in a real radio station that night, I was in heaven. Now, I was probably pitiful. I remember yelling at people, hanging up on a few callers, and generally behaving like a boor. Later, Chris told me that complaints about me flooded the station, a good sign, in a way, since it meant people were actually listening.

They hired me.

When the owner of the station, H. K. "Bud" Crowl, found out that his newest "talkmaster" was a seventeen-year-old kid who wasn't even able to master a checkbook, he made me promise that I would never, ever reveal my age on-air. In fact, I think they put that mandate in my contract.

After breaking into talk radio at this feisty little station in Dayton and putting in the first four years of my professional life there, I decided to try my hand at television. The news director for the NBC-TV affiliate in Dayton, WKEF-TV, was a fan of my radio work and offered me a job. Now, this wasn't exactly a job that featured any huge journalistic skills. The opening was for a high school quiz show called *As Schools Match Wits*.

Okay, so it wasn't anchoring *60 Minutes* but it was a job in television, pretty exciting for a twenty-one-year-old kid. Besides, one of the people I beat out for the job was another Dayton radio broadcaster at the time named Dan Pugh, who went on to fame as Dan Patrick on ESPN. The quiz show led to a couple of gigs as a sports anchor/reporter, first at WKEF-TV and then at the ABC station in Dayton, WDTN-TV.

But I longed to return to talk radio. Some newcomer named Rush Limbaugh was bursting onto the national scene at that time and I remembered how much fun I had in radio. I missed it. So I started putting out some feelers and found out about an opening in South Carolina.

I had never thought about living in the South. Growing up, I hadn't ventured much farther south than Cincinnati, Ohio. When Jim Burnside and Greg Anderson offered me a job at WFBC-AM in Greenville, the five years I spent there turned into a lot more than a great radio gig.

Life was great in "the Palmetto State" personally and professionally. I found my soul mate and wife and grew and improved as a talk radio host, working hard at the business and learning everything I could to advance. I studied other shows, spending tons of time at the radio station. I also expanded my résumé by hosting *The Tiger Tailgate Show*, a Clemson and South Carolina pregame tradition heard on the Clemson Football Network. Thousands of people gather in front of a huge stage near the football stadium to hear guests, listen to bands, and get ready for the Saturday spectacle of Clemson Tiger football.

Having my own talk radio show again was a blast. Station management pretty much let me do my thing, which often included some publicity stunts. Once, a sniper on the loose had a lot of Greenville residents worried. Someone was firing a pellet gun from the woods on I-85 and hitting some cars. No one had been hurt but the community was concerned that the Greenville County Sheriff's Department had failed to find the culprit or culprits, likely some kids playing a dangerous prank.

I decided to take matters into my own hands. I arranged for a couple of huge bull's-eyes to be printed up on banners that I taped to the side of the radio station van. Boasting to the listeners that I would "flush the sniper out of his lair," I drove up and down I-85 with the giant bull's-eyes on the van, all while broadcasting live.

Motorists gave me the thumbs-up or honked their approval. The sniper (or snipers) did not make an appearance. The Greenville sheriff, Johnny Mack Brown, was not amused. I heard from a number of his deputies who told me how furious he was with me. He figured I was making his department look bad, despite my lifelong support for law enforcement.

My Greenville run, from 1989 until 1994, was a happy time as I charted a course as a husband and father and radio host. After

WFBC was sold, I heard about an opening in Albany, New York, from Larry Gorick, the sales manager who had moved there from Greenville. Radio station WGY-AM is legendary in American broadcasting, a fifty-thousand-watt clear channel powerhouse that everyone in upstate New York knows.

Albany was just a couple of hours north of the greatest city in the world, so I jumped at the move. That, too, turned into a great run when I met a guy who would become one of my closest friends, Peter Rief, a big-voiced newsman. He was an informal sidekick on our afternoon show.

He acted like a mischievous brother, always egging me into trouble. One day, there was a story in the local news about nature lovers who wanted to save an endangered butterfly called the Karner Blue. They wanted to preserve for the creatures a field that already had been targeted for commercial development.

Naturally, I was all over these misguided folks. Private enterprise is this country's bedrock and I wasn't going to let an insect stand in the way.

This standoff is a familiar scene in America. Whether it's an obscure butterfly or a snail darter or some other insect or creature, environmentalists relish shutting down construction projects in order to save them. It doesn't matter to these activists that they threaten the livelihoods of many people who are just trying to provide for their families. To the environmentalists, a goofy little blue butterfly is more important than human beings.

At Peter's urging, I pulled another stunt. Armed with a huge butterfly net, I took my microphone and went into a local field where Karner Blue butterflies supposedly lived. Fortunately for them, there were no butterflies to be seen. But I had the radio audience eating out of my hand as I described my ridiculous romp through the woods, looking for stupid blue butterflies to capture.

The environmentalists were not amused.

I was beginning to learn how to use publicity stunts as a way to promote my opinions about serious (and not so serious) subjects. Early in my career, I learned that it wasn't enough just to come into the studio armed with opinions. They had to be delivered in a compelling, enjoyable way.

The most memorable stunt in Albany came on a blustery winter night in March 1996, when the colorful Reverend Al Sharpton came to town.

Reverend Al was all fired up about New York governor George Pataki's supposed indifference to the homeless. To liberal activists like Sharpton, the government is never doing enough for the homeless. Instead of appealing to church communities, charities, and private citizens, liberals continually expect taxpayers to foot the ever-growing tab for feeding, clothing and housing the disadvantaged.

Sharpton planned a demonstration on the lawn of the state capitol building in Albany. He announced that he would spend a bitterly cold night outside in a cardboard box, along with hundreds of his supporters.

Not quite. A worker from the posh Omni Hotel in downtown Albany, not far from the capitol, tipped me off to a reservation for the Reverend Al. He had a huge luxury suite at the hotel for the very same night that he was supposed to be staying out in the cold showing the world how tough the homeless have it.

I imagined his secret plans. When the television crews left after the obligatory live shots on the 11 P.M. news, Reverend Al was going to retreat to the warmth and comfort of that Omni suite.

Not on my watch.

Appealing to my listeners, I soon had the use of a big, beautiful motor home for the night. I had a couple of giant banners made saying: MIKE GALLAGHER'S REVEREND AL WATCH. That night, I parked the motor coach right in front of Reverend Al's "cardboard box city," watching him through binoculars to ensure that he didn't beat a path to the hotel.

All night long, I broke into regular programming with frequent updates of the scene. Listeners stopped by to offer support, bring donuts, pizza and sodas. Reverend Al was not all that thrilled, but he stayed there all night, and even shared some pizza with me.

When the cameras and microphones leave, Sharpton is actually a charming, funny guy, despite his misguided ideology.

"Gallagher," he'd say to me, in that booming voice of his, "I cannot believe we are sitting in front of the state capitol in Albany, New York, eating cold pizza with each other. I must be crazy."

I just laughed and laughed, delighted that I'd forced him to stay up—and out in the cold—all night. I may have shared my pizza, but he wasn't coming into my warm motor home. He must pay for his liberal bluster.

At one point, he handed me his cell phone to say hello to his wife, Kathy, a charming woman.

"You guys and your stunts," she said to me. "Your poor wife is probably just as mortified as I am about the things our husbands do," she said, laughing as she spoke.

Despite the bitter cold, it was a fun way to spend the night.

Even with Reverend Al. I probably made it more enjoyable for him, too. Later in an interview, he proclaimed me "The Doctor of Asininity."

I had that inscribed on a nameplate for my desk: MIKE GALLAGHER, DOCTOR OF ASININITY. Only Reverend Al could come up with a title like that. I wasn't even sure "asininity" was a real word.

I'm still not, in fact.

After two years of hosting the afternoon show on WGY in Albany, I began hearing rumors that I was being considered for a job at WABC-AM in New York City, the most listened-to talk radio station in America. I started imagining what life would be like if I ever actually received a call from them. One day, that call finally came.

Most broadcasters dream all of their lives for the chance to live and work in the New York City area. It's the country's biggest and best radio and television market. When WABC program director (and good friend) Phil Boyce offered me the job there, I remember floating out of Two Penn Plaza, the huge office building that houses the legendary talk station on the seventeenth floor, and sprinting across Seventh Avenue to my hotel room. I called Denise and screamed, "Honey, this is it!!! They gave me the job!!!" Denise screamed with joy right back at me. There we were, a couple of adults, screaming and shouting back and forth at each other over the phone. It was a moment of utter joy.

When I started, the talk radio giant, Rush Limbaugh, welcomed me to the station. He strolled down to my little desk in the hallway cubicle and told me that it was the exact same spot they gave him when he first began there. "The manager of the station was a guy named Fred who just absolutely hated me," el Rushbo said to me. "He gave me this desk out in the hall and had me sit across from Lynn Samuels." (She's a longtime left-wing New York radio personality who made Jane Fonda seem like Jeanne Kirkpatrick.) He also gave me some advice: "Don't get bogged down by the consultants and critiques from management. Just be yourself."

He should know.

The two years I spent at WABC seemed like two months. The station was in a rebuilding mode after firing the sharp-tongued talk show veteran Bob Grant, a ratings powerhouse, in April 1996. Even though I was hired to do evenings, station management immediately put me in afternoon drive, Grant's former kingdom.

After one month on the job, the bosses—Phil, John McConnell, and Mitch Dolan—summoned me to their offices to promote me again; this time the slot would be in the morning drive.

I was floored. My friend Tom Leykis, a wise and savvy talk host in Los Angeles who knows everything about everybody in our business, had given me one single, ominous warning about working at WABC: "Don't *ever* do morning drive there." He explained that WABC had tried a number of different people in the morning slot and all had failed. Morning drive in New York City is the most competitive, highly charged environment in the radio business. It's potential career suicide going up against folks like Howard Stern, Don Imus, Scott Shannon and every other morning radio star that New York has to offer.

However, the salary hike for the morning slot was difficult to turn down. With four sons either in or nearing college, the healthy bounce to my paycheck would be a tremendous help with tuition. Besides, I thought, how bad could morning drive in New York City be?

Well, in this case, it was bad. Real bad. There was the living hell of trying to go to bed at 7 P.M. every evening so I could wake up at 3 A.M. Then, it seemed as if my workplace exploded like a landmine every week, a career-ending misadventure lurking in every corner, with every half-baked idea that someone just had to give a whirl.

A few weeks into my life as New York's newest morning radio host, management decided to start experimenting with the show's on-air talent. Fine with me. "Team player" should be emblazoned on my business card. But the changes they made in a compressed period of time were, at the very least, traumatic. I never knew from one day to the next if the show would continue with the same people or if one of us would be fired.

One day they decided we needed a strong news anchor who could be my "foil," a broadcaster I could interact with about the day's news stories and talk topics. I had just the man for the job. They hired my former WGY/Albany newsman and sidekick Peter Rief. We had a terrific working relationship and had become close friends over the course of the couple of years we worked together in Albany. Now, Mike and Peter were reunited, this time in the big city.

After a few months, which I thought went smoothly, management struck again. They now wanted to pair me with someone who was more "New York." On the day that Peter was to close on a new house in New Jersey (he had the check for the down payment in his pocket), they fired him.

I'll always remember when Phil Boyce came into my office to tell me that they were releasing Peter. This wasn't just a coworker; Peter was my dear friend. And I hadn't seen this coming.

Phil spoke in a serious tone of voice. "I'm sorry, Mike, and I know you're going to take this hard, but we're going to let Peter go," he said.

"Let Peter go? Peter Rief?" I asked. I couldn't believe it. "Why?"

"Because we feel that the show needs someone who is more 'New York.' Someone who has high recognition factor here."

After Phil left, I closed the door and just bawled. I couldn't believe it. That was one of my lowest and most painful moments at WABC. (Fortunately, Peter and I would eventually reunite. Today he is the *Mike Gallagher Show*'s creative services director and announcer.)

His replacement was veteran New York TV newswoman Penny Crone, then the queen of street reporters, fearless in asking the tough question.

Penny is one of the most famous faces (and voices) on the New York City airwaves. A TV reporter who specialized in police and firefighter stories, she was also known for her devotion to the New York Yankees. Gravelly voiced and spiky-haired, she's one of those originals who New Yorkers love. She and I got along great. A TV veteran, she relied on me to show her the ropes of radio. Management knew what they wanted from our partnership: I was the straight anchor-host responsible for the show's "heavy lifting," like weather, teases in and out of breaks, introducing topics and provoking discussion by giving my position on issues. Penny would chime in, adding her two cents in her colorful, unpredictable way.

Penny's, um, unpredictability during *The Mike and Penny Show* roared into view one morning when we were talking about New York state senate majority leader Joe Bruno, the powerful Republican from upstate Rensselaer County. (Remember that place; it's important for this story.)

I praised him while Penny kept shaking her head. "What's wrong, Penny?" I asked.

"I just don't like the guy," she said.

"Why not?"

"Well, I think he's a real show-off and very pretentious with his wealth."

I didn't follow her logic, which was a frequent occurrence in our radio partnership. So, I forged on.

She began muttering about Bruno flying around in his big, fancy jet. "Joe Bruno and his big jet. Bruno and his jet."

I couldn't stand it anymore. "Penny," I asked, "what in the world are you talking about? What jet?"

Glaring at me, she shot back defensively, "Well Mike, you keep saying that he rents a big private jet . . . I don't understand why the New York senate majority leader should be doing that."

Now I was truly stumped. "I said he rents a jet?" I asked. "When did I say that?"

Penny answered, and this is all on-air, remember: "You said he rents a Lear jet. You said, Joe Bruno who rents a Lear."

It took me a moment but I finally got it. "No, Penny, not Joe Bruno who rents a Lear, Joe Bruno from Rensselaer."

Some broadcasters would have become embarrassed or upset. Not Penny, which made her all the more endearing to those of us who know her. She just laughed hysterically and we moved on to another topic. She's a funny, loving, wonderful lady and I miss her dearly since we've gone our separate ways.

I was also guilty of some on-air gaffes. Unlike Penny, I do get embarrassed. One of my most miserable on-air blunders came during a friendly exchange with Alfonse D'Amato, then the Republican senator from New York.

Penny and I were doing a phone interview with the nasal-voiced D'Amato, affectionately called the "pot hole" senator for his attention to local issues. As the new kid in town, I was trying to fit into the New York City radio landscape. I knew that Senator D'Amato was fond of talking about his mother and her wonderful Italian cooking.

"How's Mama D'Amato these days?" I asked, pleasantly enough.

"Oh, she's wonderful," Senator D'Amato answered brightly.

I decided to try and sound like a New Yorker and mention a favorite Italian dish I thought Mama might cook. "The next time you see her, you should have her fix you some Pasta Fongool. I'll bet she's good at that, eh?" I proudly asked.

Without a word, Penny jumped about three feet into the air, a considerable feat since she had been sitting down. Her eyes bulged wildly at me.

The engineer and producer looked aghast, like I had just cursed, crossed an ethical line and offended millions of people. It turned out, I had. If you know Italian, you probably know that the phrase I uttered is an obscenity. What I was trying to pry from my addled brain was Pasta Fazool, the Americanized name for Pasta e Fagioli, Italy's traditional pasta and bean soup.

Hearing the curse word, Senator D'Amato rebounded well. After a few seconds of silence, he just stammered, "Well, uh, um, *no,* Mike, I don't think we'll be having any of *that* the next time I visit Mama D'Amato."

After learning how badly I had messed up, I didn't want to get out of bed or return to work for a week. Recovering from my embarrassment, I grew to love eating (and correctly pronouncing) Pasta e Fagioli.

About eleven months into the *Mike and Penny Show,* the bosses tinkered again. This time, they released Penny and teamed me with Lionel, an afternoon host who didn't use his last name. A lawyer, his wit and delivery propelled him from chronic talk show caller in Florida straight to New York radio host. So *The Mike and Lionel Show* was born.

Trouble was, Lionel didn't want to be part of anyone's team. He flew solo, or so his agents kept insisting to WABC management. A few weeks after his meddlesome agents had lobbied to put us together, they started pressuring WABC to give Lionel his own show—without me.

Man, I knew New York radio was going to be rough, but this was brutal. My dream had morphed into a daily nightmare.

A phone call with a businessman/guardian angel turned it all around for me. John Dame and his father, J. Albert Dame, had run a group of radio stations in Pennsylvania and New York. One of those stations was WGY in Albany, my old stomping ground before joining WABC.

John had always wanted to syndicate me nationally. In the midst of all this turmoil at WABC, John and I were talking on the phone, catching up, when the subject about me doing a national show came up. The Dames had sold their radio group to Clear Channel Communications and John was ready for a new chapter in his career.

Boy, so was I.

With proverbial hat in hand, I went to my WABC boss, Phil Boyce, and begged to be released from my contract. The WABC managers are a really decent bunch, and after months of discussions, they finally let me out of my deal. They graciously allowed me to broadcast a "farewell show," in December 1998, always a confirmation in radio that the talent wasn't being fired, he or she really was resigning.

The hammer fell on Lionel a few months later. He did not receive the courtesy of a farewell show. His career at WABC was over, too, but not on his terms. Since then, I've seen him at various events or conventions and he still cracks me up. He's really a funny, funny guy. He has an uncanny ability to take an event like the O. J. Simpson trial and turn it into a hilarious example of a judicial system run amok.

But he never quite understood that the station was solidly behind the two of us and we were given a fantastic opportunity there to have a great run, if he and his agents would have allowed it. Instead, they plotted to push me off the morning show, thinking the sole spotlight would be better for him.

I'm sorry it didn't work out that way and wish him well in whatever he's doing these days. As the saying goes, it probably wasn't personal. But it sure felt like it.


It seems like everyone wants to be syndicated, but the process is harder than it sounds. I had been content to be a solid local host at a successful radio station. Call it luck and good timing that I was propelled into national syndication. Now that I've been here for a little while, I can tell you that it's a hugely competitive arena, filled with scores of talented hosts vying for a limited amount of spots on available radio stations.

The talk radio explosion started with Rush Limbaugh. After four years broadcasting to huge ratings in Sacramento, California, he took his program into national syndication on August 1, 1988. While there had always been small radio stations that made a splash locally, like Dayton's WAVI, Rush's brand of irreverent, entertaining talk captivated the entire country. He was, and is, an original.

Audiences love his tongue-in-cheek pomposity and gleeful skewering of the Democrats. Remember his nickname for our wooden former vice president, "Algore?" Fawning fans who keep telling him how much they love him become "Ditto heads." He uses frequent song parodies and musical bits.

Rush's conversational style had never been heard in a national format. His coast-to-coast following spawned hundreds of talk radio stations. *Talkers Magazine,* the industry's leading trade journal, estimates that the year before Rush went national there were about 125 talk radio stations in America. Now talk radio can be heard on about 1,200 stations in this country.

Rush is a fascinating guy. In person, he's fairly shy and introverted, not at all the type of man considered the life of anyone's party. He's entirely different in person than he is on the air. While working down the hall from him at WABC, I alternated between being in awe of this talk-radio pioneer and just trying to treat him like a colleague and coworker.

After reigning as the king of talk radio for almost a dozen years, Rush suffered some major personal setbacks. In October 2001, he revealed he was suffering from an ear disease that left him deaf in his left ear and limited the hearing in his right ear. Luckily, cochlear implant surgery, the so-called bionic ear, saved his hearing and his career.

Just two years later, his former housekeeper told the *National Enquirer* that she was his connection for black-market pain pills. Authorities launched an investigation. Years of taunting and besting liberal Democrats came back to haunt Rush as the Left reveled in his legal and personal problems.

I suppose the liberals' glee over the challenges in Limbaugh's personal life was understandable, considering how he dismissed their crazy ideology over the years. But it was truly reprehensible to see them gloat. This wasn't about politics or issues. If the news reports are to be believed, it was about a man, a fallible human being, who had to face the life-changing struggle of addiction. I wonder, where did the liberals' famous compassion go? After all, aren't they the ones who supposedly care more about people than conservatives do?

However, he survived. He entered rehab and is sounding better than ever on the radio, and continues to have the most listened-to show in the country. He is a broadcasting icon, a man credited with single-handedly saving AM radio from its deathbed. Every single one of us who collects a paycheck in talk radio owes him a huge debt of gratitude.

For good or bad, talk radio is the hottest format in the entire industry. There are issues-oriented shows like mine. Advice shows. Garden shows. Sports-talk shows. Shock-jock shows that consider dirty jokes and racy humor to be ordinary fare. They appear on various syndicates and networks and I can't say I take issue with any of them. Except one. A particular radio network that has been the bane of conservatives for years. Mention three letters to many of us and we see red.

NPR.

National Public Radio is one of the most maddening examples of liberal idiocy in America. This is radio by liberals, for liberals, and features a constant stream of newscasts and reports with a decidedly left-of-center theme.

"You're being ridiculous," a liberal would say. "They are an objective and serious news network." Really? Well, considering the off-air antics of one of NPR's former superstars, their on-air bias should come as no surprise to anyone.

In the July 7, 2003, issue of the *Nation,* John Berlau reports on a speech:

> Students at the University of Kentucky were treated in early April to a fervent antiwar and anti-Bush diatribe by a national left-leaning celebrity. In an accusatory tone, the speaker claimed President George W. Bush had "offered an attractive bribe to Turkey in exchange for permission to use Turkey as a base from which to invade Northern Iraq" and charged that he had "told the rest of the world that the United States is ready to act alone in virtually every field." The celebrity railed against the press for allegedly not being as tough on Bush as it was on former president Bill Clinton, declaring: "The press didn't wait until the intern scandal to ask tough questions of Bill Clinton, so why is the incumbent getting a pass?"
>
> The long, rambling speech, . . . also bashed radio stations for playing patriotic music as the United States went to war and even for playing the national anthem. . . .
>
> Who was this celebrity? One of the febrile Hollywood left? Tim Robbins, Sean Penn, Martin Sheen? No, the author of this

rant was none other than newscaster Bob Edwards, host of Morning Edition on the "objective" National Public Radio [NPR]. . . .

This is a radio journalist who just oozes objectivity, eh? And the worst part about NPR is how they are subsidized by taxpayer dollars. To help keep them in business, public radio stations enjoy about $86 million in annual grants from federally funded groups.

It's positively absurd that Congress has authorized millions of taxpayer dollars to go into the NPR coffers, considering the liberal bias that passes for journalism there, day in and day out. Liberals like to squawk about the so-called propaganda on conservative talk radio shows. But what's a greater example of propaganda than government-subsidized programming on the radio?

One day, the American people will become fed up with NPR and Public Television being paid for on our dime. And they'll elect representatives who stand up to public broadcasting and reject the welfare state that sustains it. In the real world of broadcasting, shows like mine either succeed or fail based on how many people listen to us. In the NPR world, ratings don't matter because they'll always have the federal government around to pay their bills.

Then there's Air America, the liberals' answer to conservatives on the radio. Most of my colleagues are career radio folks. Like me, they have spent years learning the business in small and medium markets, rising through the ranks, being promoted to bigger and better stations, and getting jobs the old-fashioned way: by earning them.

Al Franken is the centerpiece of the new "liberal talk radio network," as Air America came to be known. His background included stints on *Saturday Night Live* as a writer and performer. (Remember Stuart Smalley?) Evidently, Al was also aching to express his political views and become known as a liberal voice to be reckoned with. His book, *Rush Limbaugh Is a Big Fat Idiot,* became a best seller. He went on to write other books that basically skewered any conservative Republican in his path.

Next career move: become a radio talk show host, the liberal version of Limbaugh. So some big shot investors plunked down millions to start Air America and, presto! Al Franken joins the ever-growing field of national radio hosts. The venture also has turned comedian Janeane Garofalo, former Walter Mondale speechwriter Marty Kaplan and rapper Chuck D into talk show hosts.

But Al is the star, no doubt about it. I had the dubious pleasure of sitting on a panel with him on a chilly winter night in early 2005. And I do mean it was chilly—I was the lone conservative in a roomful of liberals gathered in Midtown Manhattan to discuss talk radio and its effects on politics.

The event was held at the Museum of Television and Radio, a beautiful, state-of-the-art facility that celebrates and chronicles the broadcasting industry. To my right was journalism professor Lee Thornton from the University of Maryland. To my left (naturally) was Al. The moderator was Michael Harrison from *Talkers Magazine.* The room was full of rabid Al Franken fans who listen to his show in New York City.

It was going to be a long evening.

To begin with, Professor Thornton seemed worried about what she called the "blurred line" between talk radio shows like mine and what is supposed to be news. This is a relatively new phenomenon among liberal elitists, this angst they display about the poor dopes who enjoy talk radio and how they supposedly aren't able to tell the difference between an opinionated host and a news anchor. The implication being that talk show listeners—particularly conservative ones—are too stupid to make the distinction. And, later, a lady in the audience stood up and announced how much smarter New Yorkers were than everyone else in America because "we get so much media here" and the heartland doesn't have many choices. The entire room, Al included, nodded in agreement. Listen, I love New York, but the pomposity of the liberal New York elite amazes me.

I felt with all my heart that they were wrong. I figured I should look into this some more and see if the facts supported Professor Thornton's argument or my experience. According to *Talkers Magazine's* Talk Radio Research Project survey of the news/talk radio audience, 55 percent of listeners consider themselves Independents (while 25 percent consider themselves Republican, and a misguided 12 percent Democrat). And 70 percent have at least some college or graduate school education. It seems to me that talk show listeners are pretty smart and can make up their own minds about what they're listening to.

Anyway, to get back to the panel, clearly the highlight of the night was Al's performance. Believe it or not, I've always gotten along with Al. We've spoken at political conventions and visited in TV green rooms and he's always been friendly, chatty and amiable. Around me, he's never acted like the kind of guy who was capable of going bonkers and physically attacking a Howard Dean heckler at a campaign event, perhaps not one of Al's finest moments.

It's pretty obvious that Al is an angry guy. While the subject of that Thursday night's panel was about the impact of talk radio, all he really wanted to do was call some conservative radio hosts liars and attack the Bush administration for the Abu Ghraib prison scandal. Harrison and I, the radio guys, kept trying to steer the conversation back to the subject of talk radio. When Franken started opining about the dangers of mercury in the fish he eats, even his fans' eyes started glazing over.

But it's his anger—and his denial that he's angry—that fascinates me.

At one point after he began raising his voice while calling Limbaugh or Hannity some childish names, his lip quivering and his face turning red, I said, "Boy, Al, you're so angry."

"No, I'm not," he sniffed. "I'm not angry at all."

It's one thing for liberals to be mad about the 2004 election. I understand the sting of losing a pivotal election, looking at maps and seeing a sea of red in the U.S., and realizing that the Democratic Party is slowly but surely imploding from within. So why deny it? Why would Al Franken, the poster boy for liberalism, pretend not to be so mad? His denial suggests one of two things: Either he thinks being angry makes him look bad (he's right), or he wishes he weren't so emotional over the relatively insignificant career of being a radio host.

The reason conservative radio hosts like me have enjoyed a measure of success is because most of us aren't angry people who take ourselves too seriously. We are comfortable and confident in who we are: opinionated broadcasters. Funny thing is, when I pointed out to Al that he'd like to be the Rush or Sean of the left, he took great offense at that. Believe me, his bosses at Air America are praying for at least half the success of talk-radio powerhouses like Limbaugh or Hannity.

Al Franken might be a funny guy, a talented writer/comic and a good family man, but he just doesn't get talk radio. But if he wants to do well, he'd better figure talk radio out soon. As he clamors for radio station clearances all over the country and hopes for great ratings and revenues like the rest of us, he has joined the club. He's courting new listeners and schmoozing advertisers, as we all do.

Perhaps he's angry because he's just one of us now. He thinks he speaks the truth. But so does every other host on the air today. He believes his side to be right, as do we all. He has a microphone and an audience to play to where he can use all his powers of persuasion to speak his mind.

As I was warned he would do beforehand by someone who knows him, midway through the evening he pulled out an old *News-Max* column I wrote about how the 2004 election made liberals like him irrelevant. One of his fans in the audience, a ghastly looking woman with an oversized fur coat, stood up and demanded to know why I would write that about him while saying that every point of view on the radio should be heard, even his. I attempted to explain the difference between disagreeing with someone politically and ideologically, but wishing them well in their endeavors. I'm not sure that nuance was understood by the crowd.

But I do wish him well. The more attention that's paid to our industry, the more we all benefit. But I'd like to offer an unsolicited piece of advice to Al and the rest of the angry liberals at Air America: Try to tone down the anger and bitterness and step up the comedy. Ask Jon Stewart—it works.

I learned a lot from that Thursday night's experience. I found out that an entire roomful of liberal New Yorkers truly believe that they're smarter and better informed than everyone else in the country. I found out that Al Franken is, indeed, capable of veering into full-fledged rage at the drop of a hat. And I discovered that the sooner Al figures out he's one of us, the better off he'll do in the cutthroat world of talk radio.

If he stays mad, he'll be off the air in less time than it took Stuart Smalley to break into tears.

And he'll never be a Sean Hannity.

Smart and funny, Sean is the most successful radio host to come along since Rush, and a guy I get to call my friend. He's now frequently called "the rock star of talk radio" based on the wildly supportive fan base he enjoys. Everywhere he goes, he's mobbed by folks who love the rock-ribbed conservative from Franklin Square, Long Island.

Sean is the hardest-working guy I know. In fact, I worry about him. Each and every day, he crams two demanding, full-time jobs into a twenty-four-hour day. When he's not on the radio hosting his show on WABC in New York and syndicated nationally by ABC Radio, he's at Fox News Channel studios for his role in the prime time hit debate show, *Hannity and Colmes*. When not broadcasting, he's flying off to some city to give a speech. And during the course of the tours for his two best-selling books—*Let Freedom Ring* and *Deliver Us From Evil*—he spent more time on airplanes and in hotel rooms than anyone I know.

Yet his priority in life remains his family. He does everything he can to spend as much time as possible with Jill and the kids. He's my kind of guy. Besides being a good friend, he's been an inspiration to me as I ventured into nationally syndicated radio.

★     ★     ★

After I left WABC, John Dame and I formed the company that would syndicate *The Mike Gallagher Show*. We called it Dame-Gallagher Networks. We secured investors, hired people and built our offices and studios in the Empire State Building in Midtown Manhattan. We started with about a dozen radio stations and hit more than a hundred within a year. Everything was going so well.

Personally, my family was happy and healthy, enjoying trips to Manhattan and life at our Long Island home. Professionally, I was in a great place, doing some of the best radio work of my career and continuing to expand my duties with Fox News Channel. It finally turned into as wonderful a life as I could have ever dared to dream.

But like millions of us, on September 11, 2001, I woke up.

# 5

# THE MORNING THAT CHANGED THE WORLD

The morning of September 11, 2001, was so bright I needed my sunglasses while driving into Manhattan on the Long Island Expressway. Nicknamed the world's longest parking lot, traffic on the expressway moved surprisingly well that September morning.

I had planned an upbeat show for that day featuring *Broadway on Broadway,* stage stars who dance and sing in Times Square. I had interviewed several of them that prior weekend, including Bebe Neuwirth, known to millions as Lilith from *Cheers,* and Brooke Shields. Being a theater junkie, I was looking forward to sharing the songs and tap dancing with my listeners.

As usual, I arrived in my eighteenth-floor office at the Empire

State Building at about 7:15 A.M. There was a fairly routine process that happened every day, no exception that morning: I touched base with my colleagues, producer Ron Mitchell and operations director Eric Hansen, two terrific young husbands and fathers who are as devoted to their families as they are to their jobs.

I finished my show prep work by around 8:50 A.M. and started doing some last-minute paperwork, checking e-mails and reading some snail mail. Moments before 9:00 A.M., Ron burst into my office screaming, "Something terrible has happened at the World Trade Center. You'd better come and look at this."

By air time, there was only one opening possible: "An unbelievable tragedy has occurred and I'm stunned," I told my listeners. ". . . a plane has crashed into the World Trade Center in New York City, in the lower part of New York City. It is devastating and it looks like it might be a passenger plane."

I became a somber news anchor, struggling to describe the horror unfolding just a couple of miles south.

"Oh my God . . . there are explosions."

The second plane hit. Now it seemed like this wasn't an accident at all. My voice rose; I was practically shouting.

"It almost appears to be—this is all speculation—but almost some kind of terrorist attack. I don't want to jump the gun here because this is all just coming in, but it appears that two different planes have struck the World Trade Center towers."

Total chaos. As I struggled to try and make sense of it all, fire alarms blared throughout the 103-story Empire State Building, triggering red strobe lights that pulsated in our offices.

"I think we're going to have to begin to evacuate the building," I said on the air. "I'm not really sure what we're going to do, it's my intent to try and stay on the air for as long as we can . . . but if we're really under attack here in New York City, I imagine they'll make us leave the Empire State Building."

As we watched television shots of the towers crumbling, a personal drama began to consume us. Through frantic phone calls from our wives and friends, we learned that two of my radio network's executives were on airplanes headed to different parts of the country. Both these men, Greg Anderson, the president of Salem Radio Network, and John Dame, the vice president of affiliate relations, are trusted friends of many years.

Off the air, during breaks, I kept calling their wives, to see if they had heard anything.

"Linda, do you know what's happening? They've flown a couple of commercial airplanes into the Twin Towers—have you heard from Greg?"

"Emily, where was John flying to? Have you heard from him? What time was he leaving?"

(Luckily, they were both safe, we learned later.)

Our panic, fear and dread almost overwhelmed us. The Empire State Building security guards began pounding at our door, demanding that we evacuate. For one brief moment I started to argue, thinking I should somehow try to stay on the air. One glance from Ron and Eric and I stopped protesting. All three of us had anxious families at home and we realized that there was a more important priority than that particular broadcast.

Gathering up some equipment, the three of us silently rode the elevator down to the lobby. Out on Fifth Avenue, we saw stunned crowds staring at the fireball in the sky. People stood open-mouthed. The wreckage loomed dead south, filling the horizon with flakes of cement, flames and smoke. It was just so unbelievable and with no frame of reference, I thought how it reminded me of the disaster movie, *Independence Day*, where stunned New Yorkers watched as aliens destroyed Manhattan. I knew that space creatures weren't blowing up New York on that bright September morning. But another type of vermin was.

In a thoughtless, intrusive reaction, I grabbed a tape recorder and microphone from Eric and started interviewing people. I've always hated those TV reporters who thrust cameras and microphones into people's faces at tragedies, asking the inane question, "How do you feel?" But I wanted to take some action just to stop feeling so useless and confused.

And scared.

One man told me he had just flown into New York City that morning from Boston, the airport where two of the doomed flights originated. "I can't believe I could have been on a plane that crashed into the Twin Towers," he said. "What in God's name could have happened up there? Has everyone gone insane?"

Insanity seemed contagious. We soon learned that the kamikaze pilots believed in the fanatical and evil Osama bin Laden, who was crazy and cunning enough to kill 3,057 innocents. Then in the ensuing weeks and months, it seemed to me that certain Americans promulgated their own form of craziness.

That moronic TV personality, Bill Maher, bestowed the virtue of courage on those nineteen evil hijackers. Imagine giving any praise to those fanatics who slit the throats of flight attendants to turn those planes, filled with innocent passengers, into missiles.

"We have been the cowards, lobbing cruise missiles from 2,000 miles away," he said on his nightly ABC-TV talk show. "That's cowardly. Staying in the airplane when it hits the building—say what you want about it, it's not cowardly."

And we thought only the terrorists were nuts. Here was a commentator, reaching millions of viewers, who actually defended the honor of those murderers. Bill Maher's brand of liberal lunacy occupied a league all its own.

Amazingly, some people rushed to his defense. After all, he was only voicing his opinion, they said. He's a risk-taker, a man who expresses what many only dare think. Well, in my opinion, anyone who thinks those terrorists showed courage hails from a mental ward or, more likely, from a Middle-Eastern enclave where hatred for the United States runs deep.

To ABC's credit, they fired Maher for his despicable comments. Yet he bounced back and gained other undeserved platforms. Now he makes money on HBO, appears on *Larry King Live* and pontificates to anyone dumb enough to listen.

And how about Congresswoman Barbara Lee? That nutty Californian, whose district covers her home city of Oakland and Berkeley, became an infamous footnote in the history books.

On September 14, 2001, the U.S. Congress empowered President Bush to marshal "all necessary and appropriate force" to hunt down the terrorists who ambushed us. The resolution passed 98 to 0 in the Senate and 410 to 1 in the House of Representatives. The lone dissenter: Barbara Lee. A Democrat, naturally.

"September 11th changed the world," she said on the House floor. "Our deepest fears now haunt us. Yet I am convinced that military action will not prevent further acts of international terrorism against the United States.

"I know this use-of-force resolution will pass although we know that the president can wage a war even without this resolution. However difficult this vote may be, some of us must urge the use of restraint. There must be some of us who say, let's step back for a moment and think through the implications of our actions today—let us more fully understand its consequences."

What was she waiting for? An invitation from the evildoers to wage war? If ever there was a time for action, not Lee's hesitation, it was in the fall of 2001.

The madness in the post-9/11 season seemed to spread from the famous to some regular folks. Kathy Hoeth, head librarian at Florida Gulf Coast University in Naples, Florida, decided to wage her own little war against patriotic displays after 9/11.

People found comfort in flying American flags and wearing patriotic pins after the terror attacks. Kathy Hoeth worried that students or faculty wearing pins that said I'M PROUD TO BE AN AMERICAN would offend foreign students on the picturesque campus. So she did what came natural to any red-blooded American liberal idiot: she banned them. The controversy was felt all over America. Outraged people everywhere sent letters, e-mails and faxes to the university.

After two days, thankfully, the university president had enough sense to reverse the ban. Once again, it was safe to wear little pins proclaiming pride in our country, even in Kathy Hoeth's library.

September 11, 2001, shattered the norms, changed your life and mine forever. The enemy brought their fanatical war into our country, slaughtering thousands of Americans. This wasn't some car bomb or act of terror on the other side of the world. This outrage happened in New York, Washington, D.C., and a Pennsylvania field.

Do you remember how united we were in the months after that awful morning? I do. As host of a partisan radio talk show, it was a relief to stop harping about the Democrats. It was liberating to view the world from the perspective of *Us* versus *Them*. It was refreshingly simple. We were Americans—people of all political stripes, from all generations, of all races and creeds. The terrorists were the enemy, fanatics who believe it was justifiable to kill 3,057 innocent men, women and children. For months afterward, we were truly the United States of America.

For the first full week after the terror attack, I had to do my daily radio show from the basement of my Long Island home. The Empire State Building remained closed and it was impossible to reach other Manhattan studios. Those first few days passed in a blur. My wife Denise said I walked around like someone lost in a fog. I worked, but without passion and verve. Detached. Morning, noon and night, I stayed behind my little desk in the basement, either doing my radio show or giving interviews to the hosts throughout the country on our radio network.

Stuck in the basement, I was only dimly aware of my family upstairs, weeping, stressed-out and worried. Our twin sons, Matt and Micah, were seniors in high school at the time. Our home in Manhasset, on the North Shore of Long Island, was a commuter town. Most people had jobs in Manhattan, many at the World Trade Center. It turned out that our little community lost forty-four people on September 11, including current residents and those who had grown up in Manhasset.

I'm not proud that I spent that first week consumed by the need to do my job, to try and make sense of this seismic shift in America and the world. I should have devoted more time to holding my wife and comforting my sons. Over the course of my career, I have often leapt into "broadcaster" mode. Some newsworthy event breaks, and I concentrate on my on-air performance. Considering the enormity of 9/11, I should have put my family first. It will always be one of my great regrets.

Looking back, my only solace is that many of our shows in those weeks served the public. One standout program featured Mary Schiavo, the former U.S. Transportation Department inspector general who resigned in 1996, exasperated over lax security at airports and on flights.

From the broadcast of September 17, 2001: "Mary, why the reluctance (to install entry-proof cockpit doors in our commercial airplanes)? Why has it been so tough?" I asked. "Why didn't anyone stand up all these years and say instead of spending all this money on new types of seats for first class, how about spending money on making airline travel safe?"

"How right you are, there's been no will to do that," she answered.

From September 20, 2001: "There's no excuse that the door to my office is more secure than the door to the cockpit of a 767," I said. "Now we've got thousands of people killed because the airlines didn't want to pay what it cost to fortify cockpit doors and keep Mohammed with a box cutter out of the cockpit."

The terrorist attack also opened up the sticky issue of racial profiling. After all, these weren't blond-haired, blue-eyed Swedes who boarded those airplanes and slaughtered thousands. In fact, every single hijacker fit a single, simple profile: young Middle-Eastern men. So after we realized what we were up against, why not begin giving more scrutiny to young Middle-Eastern men who were boarding commercial airplanes?

Naturally, the American Civil Liberties Union, or ACLU, went bonkers at the mere suggestion of such profiling. But the truth is, police officers have been using racial profiling techniques for decades. It's not something that most law enforcement agencies like to share with the public, but it's true. I've seen it, up close and personal.

For years, I've participated in police "ride-alongs," where civilians accompany an officer on patrol. As a radio host immersed in many topics involving police/community relations, it's been an invaluable tool as I've learned to see things from a police officer's perspective. I've spent literally hundreds of hours, often during the middle of the night, riding with officers in different parts of the country.

It's no secret that drug trafficking flourishes in poor, run-down neighborhoods filled with housing projects usually, if not exclusively, home to African Americans, Hispanics and other minorities. Much of the time I spent with the police was in these communities while undercover officers, often in high-tech vans, would monitor activity to capture drug buyers and sellers.

If a shiny new BMW with a young white kid would come rolling into the neighborhood, it didn't take a criminologist with a master's degree to figure out that he was probably driving around trying to score some drugs. That person was immediately scrutinized and watched very closely by the police, and inevitably busted as he began to buy drugs.

What was used to target that hapless young lad in the expensive new car? Profiling. Racial profiling, because it was the sight of a white kid in an all-black or Hispanic neighborhood that drew the officers' attention in the first place.

On a worldwide scale, the idea of scrutinizing Middle-Eastern men who might continue to board airplanes and turn them into flying death machines shouldn't be such a bad idea, even for the ACLU. It's actually a good idea for anyone who cares about America because 9/11 has completely changed the political landscape. We have to be tough as a nation and flex our muscle against our enemies—before they catch us unawares again. Our very lives depend on it.

President Bush understands this. I don't ever remember feeling prouder to be an American and a Bush supporter than when the bombs started dropping in Kabul and later in Baghdad. I imagine it was the same feeling that Americans felt when President Truman made the tough choice to use the nuclear bombs on Hiroshima and Nagasaki, which ended World War II.

With President Bush's actions, we were living up to our position in the world as the superpower that had the ability to defeat the bad guys. We knew how to take care of business. His pre-emptive strike against Iraq was and is justified for our national security.

So why couldn't every American get it? The opposition to the war on terror was maddening. It didn't seem to matter to liberal opponents of President Bush that men and women from all walks of life were willing to put their lives on the line for this just and noble cause.

Critics of the administration know and understand why we invaded Iraq. They just don't admit it. Most arguments they've used against the war are specious. Did Saddam Hussein possess weapons of mass destruction? Of course he did. Remember what happened to the Kurds? America's position would have been stronger, yes, if we had found those WMDs after invading. But history and our best intelligence at the time supported the notion that Saddam had stockpiled those weapons.

I suppose living and working in and around New York City on September 11, 2001, has made me so passionate about the war on terror. Often callers to my talk show who hail from Seattle, Washington, or State College, Pennsylvania, seem unmoved about our efforts to make the world safer. But it's an immediate cause for those of us who saw the Twin Towers burning with our own eyes or smelled the debris for days and weeks or joined the funeral processions for months afterward.

The reasons for invading Iraq and toppling Saddam Hussein's evil and dangerous regime are so obvious. We didn't start the war, Islamic terrorists did. Shortly after President Bush realized the full impact of what happened on 9/11, he reportedly said, "This is war, somebody's got to pay." Liberals think that's reckless. Our side believes it's the perfect response by our commander in chief. September 11 was war, not some isolated act. America wasn't going to sit around and wait for more bloodshed and terror on our soil.

I've often thanked God that George W. Bush occupied the Oval Office in September 2001. Only He knows how Al Gore would have reacted, but I have a strong feeling it would have included a heavy dose of the United Nations and not much in the way of military might. As much as Senator John Kerry said he would be tough on America's behalf, I also thanked God again for the results of the 2004 election.

It was easy to second-guess all that happened on that awful September day. We all nimbly jumped to conclusions, eager to uncover mistakes, like our lack of preparedness. I mentioned this before but it's worth saying again: a blessing did emerge—we were all grieving, praying, thinking as Americans. We were together. We were the United States of America.

I long for the day when we will feel united again. And I'm confident that time will return. Our American spirit grows. We are tough. We may argue and bicker, but ultimately we understand that we live in the strongest, greatest country in the world.

We still have crackpot television personalities, out-of-touch politicians and clueless bureaucrats. They've always been part of the sound and the fury of the American dialogue. We're stuck with folks like Bill Maher and Barbara Lee.

Fortunately, we outnumber them.

# 6

# THE MIRACULOUS 2004 ELECTION

No way was George W. Bush going to win in 2004.

All the mud, the money from the liberal elite establishment, the disdain from the out-of-touch liberal media—all that could be thrown at George W. Bush was thrown at him. If Hollywood wasn't attacking him with blockbuster motion pictures like *Fahrenheit 9/11,* the radio industry was rolling out an entire talk radio network, Air America, with the sole intent of defeating him. Liberal columnists like Molly Ivins and Maureen Dowd hammered the Bush administration on a daily basis, relentlessly attacking him from his policy in Iraq to his support for adviser Condoleezza Rice, later to make history as the first black woman chosen for U.S. secretary of state.

He was a rogue cowboy, they said. He was a simpleton. He

wasn't smart enough to get the job done. He stole the first election, in 2000. He just got the job because of his daddy.

Well, George H. W. Bush didn't have a whole lot to do with the election of 2004. The people spoke. And somehow, the well-financed liberal attack machine was completely shut out and shut down in November of 2004. It was nothing short of a miracle.

For millions of us, it gave us hope. But for a while there we were worried.

By the summer of 2004, those of us who support President Bush were growing concerned. The polls weren't particularly encouraging and the onslaught of Democratic pit bull dogs, led by the chief pit bull himself, John F. Kerry, kept trying to smear the president.

The 2004 campaign seemed like an episode of the *Twilight Zone.* Somehow, Senator Kerry, a man with the U.S. Senate's most liberal voting record who returned from Vietnam in 1971 as a fierce, antiwar activist, managed to convince millions that he was a prowar, mainstream American who supported the troops and the war on terror. He spouted off like this while also reminding us that he was against the war since President Bush initiated it. He voted against an $87 billion appropriations bill to give the troops much-needed weapons and ammunition, which to me showed his clear lack of support for our soldiers and their families. And while professing a disdain for negative campaigning, he attacked just about every aspect of Bush's character, variously referring to him as a liar, a cheat and a man who shirked his duties to America while serving in the Texas Air National Guard.

It was unbelievable.

I know that everyone expects conservatives like me to routinely criticize a liberal Democrat like John Kerry. But this time around, it was really deeper than that. We just couldn't believe how awful a candidate John Kerry was. Seeing the Democrats choose such a baggage-carrying presidential nominee underscored the Party's desperate position, showed how out of touch with mainstream America they are.

The results proved this. Bush won 51 percent of the popular vote compared to Kerry's 48 percent. The country was awash in red states, giving Bush 274 electoral votes to Kerry's 252.

After the closeness of the 2000 election, this one was almost like a good old-fashioned landslide. In fact, check out the state-by-state breakdown of those who voted for Bush and those who voted for Kerry.

That sea of red is more than just evidence of the reelection of George W. Bush. It's an affirmation of all the values I've been writing about in this book. Americans waded through the cesspool of empty Democratic rhetoric, scare tactics, threats to seniors, minorities and the middle class, and gave President Bush a mandate. The 2004 election was a bellowing, enthusiastic message from the voters that we were tired of the Carter/Clinton/Kennedy/Kerry brand of leadership. In his second term, George W. Bush will continue what he's been doing his entire political career: defy expectations. He'll achieve stunning victories on issues like Social Security reform, tax decreases and, most importantly, the war on terror.

Four more years. No one seemed to see it coming, least of all, the pollsters.

The exit polls were a complete and utter disaster in the 2004 election. In fact, exit polling in 2004 became the dreaded dimpled chads of 2000. The polling was downright laughable. So was the postelection defensiveness of pollster John Zogby, as he demonstrated during a contentious interview with me on my radio show.

A pollster since 1984, Zogby touts himself as "the hottest pollster in the United States today" on his Web site. His media clients have included Reuters and NBC and corporations like Coca-Cola and Microsoft. Press accounts identify him as an "independent pollster."

A few nights before the election, I watched Zogby on *The Daily Show* with Jon Stewart on Comedy Central. I try to catch Stewart's show as much as possible. While it's apparent that he's a liberal Democrat, he's an otherwise smart, funny, quick-witted guy with an entertaining program.

There was John Zogby, making a confident prediction that

Kerry was going to win the election, much to the delight of the screaming, cheering youngsters in Stewart's audience. It didn't make any sense to me that Zogby would be making the TV talk show rounds prior to the election, publicizing a prediction like this. After all, his own Web site warned about the perils of pollsters like him making incorrect predictions.

"My polling was right," Zogby said in a postelection statement entitled "Mea Culpa: I am a Pollster, Not a Predictor." He continued, "My ability to predict was wrong. For those of you who have supported my work over the years, I apologize. I will do better next time: I will just poll, not predict."

So why did John Zogby stray from polling into predicting? My hunch is that he's just another liberal Democrat who relished the chance to try and tilt the election away from George Bush. But I wanted to ask him myself. A few days after the election, I got my chance on my radio show when my producer managed to book Zogby. And let's just say we had a very lively exchange.

While he was on hold, I issued a quick apology on-air about an unrelated issue. The Lance Armstrong yellow-bracelet phenomenon had just started spreading in America at the time. Earlier in the year, I made some passing comments about how I would never wear the yellow bracelet since I saw John Kerry sporting one. Realizing how petty and short-sighted that opinion was, I said that I was sorry for having denigrated such a worthwhile cause as Armstrong's foundation that promotes cancer research. (This is important to remember as you read on and gauge Zogby's reaction.)

ME: John, [there's a] lot of anger over your comments predicting pretty confidently that John Kerry would win.

ZOGBY: Yeah.

ME: Well how do you—

ZOGBY: So what's your question?

ME: How do you have any credibility, Mr. Zogby, I mean, how can—

ZOGBY: Well, my polls were dead-on.

ME: —you have any credibility left after you made the talk show rounds predicting that John Kerry would win?

ZOGBY: Credibility? My polls were dead-on and I made a projection on the basis of a trend that I saw, posted a statement on my Web site, Mike.

ME: I'm curious about something. I know that you're based in Utica and I was reading an article in the *Utica Observer-Dispatch,* I guess. You conceded, "I'm not a predictor, I'm a pollster. I made a prediction; it just goes to show I don't have a crystal ball." Well, then, why did you act like a predictor?

ZOGBY: I don't understand where you're coming from. I made a prediction and obviously—did that move the stock market? Did anybody die from it?

ME: No, I think, though, that—

ZOGBY: Did it change the course of the election?

ME: I think—

ZOGBY: Did it hurt anyone?

ME: It could very well—

ZOGBY: Did it cause you to go into a fetal position?

ME: No, I think what it probably did is maybe cause some people not to vote because a so-called—

ZOGBY: Oh, stop that.

ME: —respected pollster like John Zogby said that it was in the bag, Kerry was going to win.

ZOGBY: Find me five people who didn't vote and then we'll have this conversation.

ME: Well, we'll find lots of people.

ZOGBY: That's silly.

ME: There are a lot of people who didn't vote. I mean, John, with all due respect, I think the role of a pollster first of all, I think everybody's agreeing that the, specifically the exit polling, has just been thoroughly discredited this year. And people are disgusted with the role of some of these polls. But what worries me specifically, I saw you on television, I watched you on Jon Stewart's show, for crying out loud. Millions of young people are watching and you made your very confident prediction that John Kerry would win. I mean, with all due respect, you don't think that that kind of a prediction from a supposedly respected pollster could influence a voter who's going to the polls?

ZOGBY: Well, did it?

ME: I don't know!

ZOGBY: Well, did it?

ME: I don't know! Maybe it did.

ZOGBY: Did it go from my lips to a Kerry victory?

ME: Hey, maybe Kerry voters didn't vote for him because John Zogby said it, it was a foregone conclusion that he was going to win. I don't know.

ZOGBY: I think you ought to go back to the bracelets.

ME: Well, naw. I'd like to talk about the pollsters. I mean, when did you, have you always sort of made the rounds—

ZOGBY: Better make it quick, cause you've got about thirty seconds. I told the producer that you'd get five minutes.

ME: Well, I think we've had three, so then we've got two more minutes. But with all due respect, have you always kind of been this sort of quasi-celebrity who made the rounds and made predictions before the election? Or have you just been really focused on data?

ZOGBY: You're starting to blubber and blather a little bit. Ask me about the polls. My polls were dead-on. We got the polls correct in pretty much every state except those where we were fifty-fifty and it was too close to call. And then I in turn made a prediction and again I don't know of anybody who's in the hospital or is being buried today because I made a prediction. I issued a statement about the prediction where I thought I saw a trend and the trend didn't materialize. I thought there'd be a lot of young voters. We all did, frankly.

ME: Any predictions of a career change for John Zogby, now that you blew this so badly this year?

ZOGBY: Oh, I might have a syndicated radio show talking about Lance Armstrong and bracelets maybe.

ME: Pretty good topic, cancer benefits. Cancer survivor support is a good thing, don't you think?

ZOGBY: Well, you attacked them though, didn't you?

ME: I didn't only attack them, I apologized for it today. And I appreciate you acknowledging it. Maybe you'll apologize for being so wrong about the 2004 election.

ZOGBY: No need to apologize. I wasn't as crass as you were about a cancer victim. Um. I've given you plenty of time. You've had a lot of fun with this. Come to my Web site, Zogby.com—

ME: Nawwh, I think we're not interested in coming to your Web site—

ZOGBY: Mike, thank you so much for this final conversation.

ME: Good luck with your career as a radio host.

ZOGBY: Thank you so much for this final conversation, now that we know who you are.

ME: Maybe you'll do better as a radio host—

ZOGBY: Bye, Mike.

ME: —than you are as a pollster.

ZOGBY: Bye, Mike, you can talk about me, now that I'm gone. Bye. (Click.)

The "click" of Zogby hanging up the phone was music to my ears. By cutting short the interview, it was apparent that he felt so boxed into a corner by my legitimate questions about the role of a high-profile pollster like him. He just tucked tail and ran, and could not own up to his bias.

The listener e-mails came pouring into the studio.

What an absolute jerk!!! John Zogby just crashed and burned on national radio, Mike. I can't believe the arrogance, the anger, the bitterness, and the downright incompetence of a guy like him. And you exposed him for the phony he is.

    Carol

I've always wondered why I've never gotten called by a pollster, Mike. Now I guess I know. The fierce liberal agenda that a guy like Zogby perpetuates on an unsuspecting public is hardly scientific. Zogby should have taken his medicine and accepted your justifiable criticism. Instead, he lashed out at you like a spoiled little brat.

    K. L.

Gallagher, tell me that wasn't really John Zogby, the feared and heralded pollster. That guy sounded like a dweeby little brat who met his match in you. Go ahead, come clean, and admit that it was some imposter. Surely John Zogby wouldn't come off that poorly in a radio interview . . .

    Lynne

Perhaps the victory of President Bush in 2004, not to mention the gains in the House and Senate, will also be remembered for the overwhelming failure of exit polls and supposed polling "experts" like John Zogby.

Other than stoking their fierce competitive fires, hypothetical scenarios or data that turn out as faulty as the 2004 polling numbers, should never influence potential voters. There is nothing accomplished by networks trying to rush to the airwaves with polling data before the polls even close or the votes can be counted.

No American should be exposed to a smarmy, arrogant pollster like John Zogby trying to impress a college-aged TV crowd on a talk show by projecting victory for a candidate who would ultimately get soundly defeated. It's time to turn away from the hyperkinetic polling crowd and just let elections be determined the good old-fashioned way: by the voters.

After the votes were counted and the Republican victories were assured, I debated Democratic strategist Sascha Burns on Fox News Channel. I asked her if she remembered the song from the long-running Broadway musical *Les Misérables* called "Do You Hear the People Sing?"

The people are singing. We're singing a song of determination and resolve. All of them: Michael Moore and Al Franken and Molly Ivins and Frank Rich and Barbra Streisand and Dan Rather and Ted Kennedy and Terry McAuliffe and Sean Penn and George Soros and the rest of the Democratic machine, threw everything they could at America's commander in chief.

But the Democratic machine broke down and failed.

Americans are fed up with the tired old liberal philosophy of the past. We're through with the hopelessness of presidential campaigners who are more interested in attacking their opponents than in giving reasons to vote for their guy.

The fight continues. If it's true that political power is just a swinging pendulum, the Democrats will get their chance again. Liberals are licking their wounds and strategizing for the next election. But the 2004 election was a solid rejection of the liberal stranglehold that has held on for a number of years.

This time, the idiots lost.

# 7

# AMERICA LOVES A FAIR AND BALANCED NETWORK

Dan Rather's forty-five-year broadcasting career has been slanted by his liberal bias. This supposedly objective journalist would bait, taunt and criticize conservative Republicans every chance he'd get.

Americans got their first glimpse of what would be decades of biased behavior from Rather when they watched his exchange with President Richard Nixon at a 1974 press conference. Responding to the murmurs and jeers from other reporters during a particularly feisty exchange, the president asked, "Are you running for something?" Rather answered, "No sir, Mr. President—are you?"

And Dan was just getting started.

In 1988, Rather was at it again, revealing his anti-Republican bias as he hammered away at George H.W. Bush, the vice president.

Rather kept interrupting the vice president in a testy exchange about the Iran-contra scandal. It was a contentious live interview that brought a flood of viewer complaints to CBS. Rather was also criticized by his colleagues. Sam Donaldson said, "Rather went too far." And Mike Wallace, a fellow CBS correspondent said, "The style was wrong. Dan lost his cool."

These stunts by Rather were just the most obvious expressions of the slanted, liberal reporting that has colored his too-long career. Today, millions of us have come to recognize Rather as a symbol of the media elite, the highly paid group of arrogant, left-leaning electronic journalists who hold conservatism in contempt and disdain.

After years of reigning as one of the most powerful forces in American journalism, Dan Rather's career came crashing down in the fall of 2004, in the uproar over apparently forged documents about President George W. Bush's Vietnam-era National Guard service. CBS aired a false story suggesting that Bush enjoyed cushy treatment in his military service just six weeks before the presidential election. Rather's blatant and shoddy attempt to sway voters against the president exploded in his face.

After initially sticking by its obviously flawed story, CBS admitted its error ten days later. In a stunning retraction, the network said it was "deliberately misled" about the authenticity and source of those documents. Rather apologized on the air.

An independent panel assembled to investigate the debacle found that the National Guard report should never have been aired. In the wake of the scandal, CBS fired the producer of the segment and demanded resignations from three other news executives. Rather conveniently announced his retirement as anchor six weeks before the panel's findings, so he was spared further punishment.

So Dan Rather was out.

And Fox News Channel was definitely in.

In October of 1996 when Roger Ailes launched a twenty-four-hour all-news cable network, the snickers from the liberal elite could be heard in newsrooms all over America. That's because a liberal bias has reigned supreme for years on the major networks—ABC, NBC and CBS. And the network created by Ted Turner, CNN (the "Clinton News Network" to many conservatives) had set the standard for the way cable news would work. Nearly a decade later, the joke is on them, though. And I'm not sure that even Roger Ailes could have predicted the kind of success Fox has enjoyed.

The Fox News Channel motto is its foundation: Fair and Balanced. Besides great worldwide news coverage featuring experienced and skillful reporters, the opinion and talk shows on Fox offer both sides of political and social issues in a fast-paced style that viewers love. I should know. I work there.

As a contributor and guest host for Fox News Channel, it's my job to appear on the various shows as a "pundit"—i.e., "talking head"—or fill in for one of the hosts on shows like *Hannity and Colmes* or *Fox and Friends*. I have a pretty good feeling for the way they operate, ideologically speaking.

As I mentioned earlier, their mission is to consistently present both points of view fairly and accurately. When I'm asked to give my opinion about a topic, I never appear alone; a liberal commentator is always invited to debate me. Presenting a Democrat's perspective is as important to Fox as airing a Republican point of view.

Still the Fox News Channel is constantly criticized as being some kind of a right-wing tool for the Republican Party. "But Fox isn't exactly pursuing a stealth strategy: anyone who can't figure out that it's in the tank with the Republican Party must be brain dead," wrote Frank Rich of the *New York Times* in July 2004. Consider these digs by Tom Shales of the *Washington Post* accusing Fox of bias while reporting on Ronald Reagan's funeral: "The pro-Bush Fox News Channel seemed to be playing the pomp and pageantry fairly straight, without trying to inject political subtext—although time was found for a gushy report on President Bush's meeting with the president of Iraq and how swimmingly the war was going."

Never has the contempt that liberals hold for Fox News Channel been felt more profoundly than in August 2004, when the Republican National Convention was held in New York City. New York liberals were positively apoplectic that their city would be hosting the GOP convention.

During convention week, there were numerous protests in the streets of Manhattan. Anarchists, gays and lesbians, wild-eyed environmentalists, you name it, all seemed intent on disrupting the convention. As one liberal activist put it, "We're going to make life miserable for every single Republican delegate who is here."

On the afternoon of President Bush's acceptance speech, I was at the corner of Thirty-third Street and Fifth Avenue, in front of the Empire State Building, when the police erected orange mesh barricades to keep people from crossing the street. This is a routine precaution for VIP motorcades. This time, a police officer told me, it was going to be *the* motorcade—the president's.

Great, I thought, I'm in the right place to watch the presidential motorcade and all the attendant hoopla. With briefcase in hand, wearing a Fox News Channel golf shirt, I stopped and waited for our commander in chief to drive by. My good mood evaporated, though, when a man standing next to me began screaming.

"You Fox-News Nazi," the balding man with wild eyes bellowed at me. "How dare you stand on my street, you Fox-News Nazi!"

Wonderful. Police barricades pressed in front of me while crowds straining to see the president crowded behind me. I was trapped like a lobster in a net. In this tight space, I was now stuck with a crazy man.

"I want you Fox-News Nazis to leave my city and leave it now," he ranted. "You have no business here. You are a bunch of right-wing extremists who should be shot."

Swell. Now he wanted us shot.

Finally the police motorcycles arrived, signaling the start of the long line of limousines in the president's entourage. The ranting and raving man with a filthy shirt turned his wrath on President Bush.

"I hope you die, George Bush!" the man screamed. His words caused people to shift uncomfortably. "Someone needs to put a bullet between his eyes, I tell you." As this psycho revved up, veins bulged around his temples and he began to sweat. I was really worried that this guy could hurt someone.

Meanwhile, President Bush's limousine passed, the crowd applauded, cheered and waved. This reception made the crazy man even crazier.

"You bunch of stupid Nazis," he shrieked. "How can you cheer for a monster like Bush?"

The president's car drove past and we glimpsed George W. Bush in the backseat, waving at us. We waved back enthusiastically, still pelted by the ravings of a liberal lunatic who thinks *we're* the crazy ones. Eventually the motorcade passed by, police removed the barricades, and the nut disappeared into the Midtown Manhattan crowd, another angry liberal idiot in a sea of humanity in the biggest city in America.

★　　★　　★

What infuriates liberals, even quiet types, is America's migration to the Fox News Channel. More and more viewers are turning away from other television networks and tuning into Fox in droves. On the final night of the Republican National Convention, television history was made. For the first time ever, a cable news network beat each of the "big three"—CBS, NBC and ABC—in the ratings. Fox's ratings were huge on election night as well.

In the November 8, 2004, *New York Times,* reporter Jacques Steinberg wrote: "Election Night 2004 delivered more than one decisive victory. . . . Fox News clobbered the other cable news networks, its 8.1 million viewers more than tripling its own election night prime-time performance in 2000. NBC, ABC and CBS, on the other hand, lost millions of viewers this year, according to Nielsen Media Research. And Fox News actually came closer to CBS in the ratings than CNN did to Fox News."

Fox News Channel is now America's leading cable news network. It routinely doubles or even triples the ratings of CNN or MSNBC. And the network continues to grow. I'm excited to be a player on its team. It feels good to be part of this television revolution. Not only can I appreciate Fox News Channel as a viewer, but I get to work there, too.

I'll continue to proudly wear a Fox News Channel golf shirt, or jacket, or T-shirt, even on the corner of Thirty-third Street and Fifth Avenue in New York City.

# 8

# THE DAY I KILLED A COW . . . I MEAN, STEER

People for the Ethical Treatment of Animals—PETA—is one of those shrill, hysterical liberal machines. They are the nuts who spray-paint fur coats. They believe it's cruel to catch fish.

"We've got extensive, extensive evidence on our Web site, which is just fishinghurts.com," said PETA spokesman Bruce Friedrich during an August 2002, *Hannity and Colmes* segment where I was the invited voice of reason.

"Biologically and physiologically, fish feel pain in the same way that dogs and cats—" the PETA man said.

When Alan Colmes seemed to swallow that line, I weighed in.

"Alan, to acknowledge that fish feel pain is the same as acknowledging that we know rats can feel pain," I said. "They're fish, Alan. The problem with this is, PETA chases away anybody who'd ever want to be part of this organization, but the only thing missing right now from Bruce is a tinfoil hat on his head."

I've also debated PETA on my radio show. On a slow news day, my producer can easily dredge up one of its spokespeople to boast about its latest escapade. PETA is sort of like the proverbial car crash: we know we're not supposed to watch, but we can't really help it.

Once I asked a PETA guest what one should do with head lice, since the organization is so fundamentally opposed to destroying any "life form." He calmly told me that a person with lice should make every effort to remove those buggers gently and delicately, without harming them. Listening to a PETA person is like overhearing chatter in a mental ward.

You should understand that I love animals, especially dogs. I've frequently contributed to various no-kill animal shelters and the Humane Society over the years. I have a hard time with people who don't like dogs, or cats or any kind of pets. My wife Denise never used to be a dog person. That's because while growing up, she just never had a dog. She had a cat named Cindy Kat, but she never experienced the complete joy of a dog. Until I found Thumper.

He was a shivering, tiny little black cocker spaniel/Labrador mix that I found at the Greenville, South Carolina, Humane Society. I have no idea why I went out to get a dog that day. Maybe it was because as a boy, I always had a dog. When I was three years old, there was Thumper the First. He, too, was a black cocker, and when he died, we got Thumper II. Now that I was a single guy, I guess I figured it was time to find Thumper III.

When I brought him home, Denise came over to my apartment

and it was love at first sight. Not only did she fall instantly in love with him, but, like me, he was drawn to her. To this day, Thumper is Denise's shadow. He follows her everywhere and loves nothing more than to get a good belly rub from her. I rescued Thumper from the pound, but he is definitely Denise's dog.

Everyone should experience a dog's unconditional love. I feel sorry for people who come home from a miserable day at the office and aren't greeted by a wagging tail or a happy lick on the hand. These days, Thumper has a little sibling, a tiny beagle named Buster. At thirteen years of age, my buddy Thumper is getting up in years. We think that five-year-old Buster, who romps and bounds and plays, keeps him young. He acts as though he just tolerates Buster, but we suspect he really loves having another dog in the house.

It's one of life's simple pleasures that pet owners—and their pets—have a knack for making each other happy. But PETA veers off the roadway in its appreciation of animals, crashing into the ditch of goofy, logic-defying activism. For instance, it ran an insensitive and medically unproven advertisement linking Rudy Giuliani's prostate cancer to milk. The National Organization for Women protested as sexist a 2000 PETA ad against fur trim in clothing. "Fur Trim Unattractive" pictured a woman's crotch with excessive pubic hair.

PETA considers these tasteless stunts "compassion in action" for animal rights. To me, it seems as though they believe animals are more important than people. PETA president Ingrid Newkirk has been famously quoted as saying that "a rat is a pig is a dog is a boy," in arguing that humans are no more special than other mammals. These screwballs really believe that. When Newkirk protested suicide bombings in a 2003 letter to Palestinian leader Yasser Arafat, she complained about militants blowing up a donkey rigged with bombs. Asked about human casualties in the Middle East, she told the *New Yorker,* "We are named People for the Ethical Treatment of Animals . . . there are plenty of other groups that worry about the humans."

I've tangled with PETA for years, although maybe not as long as people such as *Vogue* editor Anna Wintour. She landed in PETA's crosshairs for liking fur coats and showcasing them in her magazine. Well, that's her right and her publisher's, too. Women like to buy and wear furs. *Vogue* is in the women's fashion business. This is America.

PETA doesn't care. This organization and other animal-rights activists have dogged Anna Wintour for years. In 1996, a protester dumped a raccoon's frozen carcass on her table at Manhattan's Four Seasons restaurant as she ate lunch. Seven years later, PETA distributed a poster of a frowning Anna under the slogan FUR IS WORN BY BEAUTIFUL ANIMALS AND UGLY PEOPLE. PETA put these up around Manhattan just as the Council of Fashion Designers awarded her for lifetime achievement.

Red pawprints and the slur FUR HAG spray-painted on Anna's Manhattan brownstone led to a $50 million civil suit. To add insult to injury, the editor's nanny claimed brain damage from fumes of the paint thinner used to clean the graffiti. She sued *Vogue's* parent company and the cleaning contractors, settling for $2.2 million in 2004.

Although Anna Wintour may be a pampered "fashionista" with an icy reputation (nickname: Nuclear Wintour), she deserves our sympathy. She's suffered enough from the animal nuts. Go away, loonies. Leave the poor woman alone.

In 2000, a PETA stunt outraged me. The organization launched an advertising campaign encouraging young people, eighteen and nineteen-year-old college kids, to drink beer instead of milk. PETA decided it was time to stop milking cows because it was too upsetting and uncomfortable for the creatures. I'm no veterinarian, but I'm pretty sure that cows suffer if they are never relieved of milk they're carrying, right?

PETA kicked off an outdoor billboard and magazine campaign spoofing the dairy industry slogan "Got Milk?" by replacing it with "Got Beer?" PETA placed these "Got Beer?" ads in college newspapers and university communities. It was as if they never heard of the nationwide epidemic of teenagers who drink, drive and die. Mothers Against Drunk Driving blasted PETA for promoting underage drinking and the organization subsequently pulled the ads.

I am extremely sensitive to the devastation alcohol abuse wreaks in America. Alcoholism destroyed one of my closest friends, turning his life into a spiral of despair and failure. He died penniless, leaving behind a trail of misery—a broken, alienated family, a house lost to the bank and a sad end to a wonderful life, all from years of abusing vodka. He was a kind, caring, giving, funny guy who would spend hours with others who were perceived as hopeless. I miss Phil to this day. So when a group such as PETA recklessly and irresponsibly promotes drinking, among teenagers yet, it makes me crazy.

I decided to fight back on PETA's turf, the land of attention-grabbing stunts. Why couldn't I stage an event that would beat PETA at its own game? I announced that I would buy a cow that was scheduled for slaughter, broadcast its "execution" on my radio show and donate the beef to the homeless. Hearing this, the PETA folks went out of their minds. This had to be a little tricky for them since a bunch of hungry and needy people were going to be enjoying nice, juicy steaks and hamburgers from the slaughtered cow. But the idea of broadcasting a cow's death really drove them wild.

On the air, I told a PETA spokeswoman about my idea and the poor woman was so upset, she could barely speak. "How can you sleep at night?" she shrieked. "Have you really given any thought to what the final moments of the cow's life are going to be like with you and your microphones there?"

I could barely contain my glee. Now I just had to find a cow. That was easy, thanks to my listeners. When I explained my plans on the air, many folks called in with supportive ideas and encouraging comments. A farmer in West Virginia, David Hall, called to offer a 400-pound steer at a reasonable price, about $700. My on-air conversation with him was classic, a city boy trying to buy a cow from a farmer.

ME: David, does this cow have a name?

DAVID: Mike, it's not a cow, it's a steer.

ME: What's the difference between a cow and a steer?*

DAVID *(uncontrollable laughter)*

ME: Okay, so what's the steer's name?

DAVID *(recovering from his uncontrollable laughter):* Old Blue.

---

*Cow: "the mature female of cattle or of an animal (as the moose, elephant or whale) in which the male is called bull."
Steer: "a male bovine animal castrated before sexual maturity and usually raised for beef."
Source: *The Merriam-Webster Collegiate Dictionary,* Tenth Edition.

Old Blue. Perfect. This was getting better by the second. We even wound up with a theme song. In tribute to our mission, Pete Baum, a musician from West Virginia, wrote a ditty, "Ode to Old Blue." He played his guitar and sang it live on the air:

> *Old Blue, we're gonna miss you.*
> *I just can't wait, until you become a juicy steak.*
> *Sirloin and ribeye and T-Bone, too.*
> *Old Blue, we're gonna miss you.*
> *The ASPCA did too little too late.*
> *Just to make 'em happy, we'll give 'em a piece of steak.*
> *Old Blue, we're gonna miss you.*
> *I think that you deserve a glass of milk to calm your nerves.*
> *PETA would have been here, but we ain't got beer.*
> *Old Blue, we're gonna miss you.*
> *Do you realize, it's time for you to die.*
> *We're gonna send you up to the pasture in the sky.*
> *Old Blue, we're gonna miss you.*
> *Old Blue, we're gonna miss you.*

We had to find a place to donate beef from a 400-pound steer. A shelter run by Catholic Charities called to gratefully accept our gift, saying hundreds of homeless people would be receiving meals, thanks to Old Blue's demise. So arrangements made, we headed to Wheeling, West Virginia, to broadcast the death of Old Blue.

The day we were to leave from our New York studios, Eric Hansen burst into my office, a worried look on his face. By then, I had already received about a dozen death threats over Old Blue. The

American Humane Association criticized me as "outrageous and completely irresponsible." Some of our affiliates were growing nervous about airing the execution.

"You're not going to believe this, but there's a group of angry PETA protesters outside the office," Eric said. "They know you're headed to West Virginia and they're going to try and keep you from leaving the building."

Sure enough, about twenty-five protesters wearing Birkenstock sandals and flannel shirts blocked the lone exit from our studios in the Empire State Building. Our crack building security managed to usher those anxious animal-rights nuts outside, hustle me into a freight elevator and escort me to my car.

At that time, we used a small private plane to travel around the country, a Cessna twin-engine. We took off from Teterboro Airport in New Jersey, and headed for Wheeling. Circling around the airport before we landed, we were treated to an amazing sight: a bunch of excited people holding up signs saying WELCOME, MIKE and GOOD-BYE, OLD BLUE. Television news crews and reporters were waiting for us. This was going just the way I wanted.

The going got tougher, though, at Bledsoe's Meatpacking, the slaughterhouse in Cameron, West Virginia.

"I am a little queasy," I told my listeners.

I couldn't watch. Despite my disdain for PETA and kooky activists, witnessing the slaughter of this huge four-year-old steer bothered me.

At the "killing room," inside a cement bunker, workers typically lead a steer from a giant pen to a big, wooden brace, fitting its head inside. They then take a .22-caliber Mach, position it against the steer's head and, well, send it to that great pasture in the sky. Alas,

Old Blue refused to go quietly. He backed up, turned around and tried to walk out of the bunker.

"Oh the humanity of it all, he's made a break for it, something has happened," I announced to my listeners. "They are having trouble getting Old Blue into the cement bunker. The PETA people are going to think he's scared. Is he scared, Bill?" I asked of the slaughterhouse worker who was guiding Old Blue around by a lead around his snout.

"No he's not," said Bill, explaining that the steer wasn't used to hearing all the noise from our entourage.

To me, it was almost as if Old Blue knew his fate. It took twenty minutes for five men to push, pull and tug that steer in place. At one point, he was dragged along on his knees.

"Please promise me, this is one shot, get him done," I said. "We don't want him to linger."

I turned my head away in the last moments as a loud shot rang out. "Did he fall? I'm not looking." Indeed, he'd fallen.

"Old Blue is dead," I then announced. "Long live Old Blue's memory. We're now going to feed hundreds of hungry people throughout the Ohio Valley."

Despite the harrowing final moments, Old Blue's slaughter was a grand slam. I figured a way to get under PETA's skin and really tweak them. Our event received national attention, even in Europe, spreading the message that many Americans abhor the shock tactics of the animal rights nuts. And hundreds of needy, hungry people in the Ohio Valley received choice, grade-A beef.

Is this a great country, or what?

# 9
# FAMILY: WHAT AMERICA IS ALL ABOUT

Her laugh made me fall in love. Because when my wife laughs, all is right with my world. Denise's loud, lusty laugh is like a party invitation. You want to join in and be happy with her. Her face opens up and her eyes sparkle as she throws back her head, making the most joyous sound I've ever heard. I'm not embarrassed or shy about saying that Denise is my universe. I'd rather be with her than anyone else in the world.

I've come to treasure marriage. My life before Denise was lonely, empty and irrelevant. Remember the sappy Tom Cruise line from the movie *Jerry Maguire?* It's "You complete me." I must be the nation's biggest sap because I know exactly what he meant.

Many Americans share my feelings about the blessings marriage can bring. The institution is alive and well, thank you very much. Millions appreciate the value of a man and woman committing to a lifetime together. Despite efforts to undermine, challenge and distort marriage, it is thriving. Americans understand that marriage can bring joy and lifelong happiness. Like it or not, our nation defines marriage as being between a man and a woman.

But not everyone sees it that way.

In the May 12, 2004, *Boston Globe* there was a disturbing headline: FREE TO MARRY: HISTORIC DATE ARRIVES FOR SAME-SEX COUPLES IN MASSACHUSETTS. In the article, Yvonne Abraham and Rick Klein report the following:

> Massachusetts became the first state in the nation to permit gays and lesbians to wed just after midnight today, when Cambridge City Hall welcomed more than 250 same-sex couples who hugged, cried, cheered, and applied for the marriage licenses many thought they would never see in their lifetimes.
>
> Outside City Hall, 10,000 supporters and onlookers gathered to witness the historic event, spilling off the grounds of City Hall, and clogging Massachusetts Avenue. Police in riot gear lined the street, but the anticipated clash between protesters and supporters of gay marriage never came: All but a handful of opponents stayed away.
>
> "This is like winning the World Series and the Stanley Cup on the same day," said Susan Shepherd, 52, who, with her partner, Marcia Hams, 56, was the first to apply for a marriage license in Massachusetts. "I'm trying not to lose it. We just really feel awesome. It's awesome.

"There's a kid somewhere that's watching this," she continued, fighting back tears. "It's going to change his whole life."

What began in Cambridge last night will continue in city and town halls across the state today, as a November ruling by the Massachusetts Supreme Judicial Court granting gays and lesbians the right to marry goes into effect. The licenses are to be granted after years of legal wrangling, political maneuvering, and fractious public debate, which will probably continue even after the first gay and lesbian marriages. The giddy celebrations of couples in Cambridge last night, and those expected in other cities and towns across the state today, will soon give way to disputes over the reach and validity of same-sex marriages elsewhere in the country. . . .

When Massachusetts became the first state in America to legalize gay marriage, people reacted as if the world had ended. Some of my listeners wept as they called my radio show, airing their grave misgivings that a handful of activist judges decided gays and lesbians could be legally wed. It was a sad day in this country's history, demonstrating just how far gay activists had come in persuading judges to embrace their cause. Gay marriage has never been put to voters in a national referendum. It's only been through the courts that this monumental blunder has occurred.

Please don't misunderstand me. I respect the rights of everyone and hate discrimination in all its forms. Intolerance against gays is wrong. When gay partners commit to each other, that's fine. In fact, I think I might be open to the compromise of civil union—just so long as marriage continues to be defined as the union between one man and one woman.

Never has the "slippery slope" been better defined than with this volatile topic. If the courts have decided that marriage in America is *not* reserved for one man and one woman, there can be no stopping this freight train from steaming down the tracks, expanding into questionable arrangements. Pennsylvania senator Rick Santorum saw this one coming well before the Massachusetts Supreme Judicial Court ruled in favor of gay marriage. In an April 7, 2003, interview with the Associated Press, Santorum, chairman of the GOP conference in the Senate, said there were consequences when society allows people to express "whatever wants or passions they desire."

SANTORUM: I have no problem with homosexuality. I have a problem with homosexual acts. As I would with acts of other, what I would consider to be, acts outside of traditional heterosexual relationships. And that includes a variety of different acts, not just homosexual. I have nothing, absolutely nothing against anyone who's homosexual. If that's their orientation, then I accept that. And I have no problem with someone who has other orientations. The question is, do you act upon those orientations? So it's not the person, it's the person's actions. And you have to separate the person from their actions.

AP: . . . so if somebody is homosexual, you would argue that they should not have sex?

SANTORUM: We have laws in states, like the one at the Supreme Court right now, that has sodomy laws and they were there for a purpose. Because, again, I would argue, they undermine the basic tenets of our society and the family. And if the Supreme

Court says that you have the right to consensual sex within your home, then you have the right to bigamy, you have the right to polygamy, you have the right to incest, you have the right to adultery. You have the right to anything. Does that undermine the fabric of our society? I would argue yes, it does. It all comes from, I would argue, this right to privacy that doesn't exist in my opinion in the United States Constitution. . . . And now we're just extending it out. And the further you extend it out, the more you—this freedom actually intervenes and affects the family. You say, well, it's my individual freedom. Yes, but it destroys the basic unit of our society because it condones behavior that's antithetical to strong healthy families. Whether it's polygamy, whether it's adultery, whether it's sodomy, all of those things, are antithetical to a healthy, stable, traditional family.

Every society in the history of man has upheld the institution of marriage as a bond between a man and a woman. Why? Because society is based on one thing: that society is based on the future of the society. And that's what? Children. Monogamous relationships. In every society, the definition of marriage has not ever to my knowledge included homosexuality. That's not to pick on homosexuality. It's not, you know, man on child, man on dog, or whatever the case may be. It is one thing. And when you destroy that you have a dramatic impact on the quality. . . .

His arguments made sense. This all comes down to a basic reality: anything goes if the definition of marriage expands beyond the bond between one man and one woman. Everyone knows this truth, but many people censor themselves, fearful of repercussions. Look what happened to Senator Santorum when he pointed out the obvious.

Two weeks later, on April 21, 2003, Lara Jakes Jordan reported for the Associated Press that "gay-rights groups, fuming over Sen. Rick Santorum's comparison of homosexuality to bigamy, polygamy, incest and adultery, urged Republican leaders Monday to consider removing the Pennsylvania lawmaker from the GOP Senate leadership."

The article went on to say:

"We're urging the Republican leadership to condemn the remarks. They were stunning in their insensitivity. . . ." said David Smith, a spokesman for the Human Rights Campaign, the nation's largest gay advocacy organization. "We would ask that the leadership reconsider his standing within the conference leadership." . . .

Among the groups condemning Santorum's remarks were the Center for Lesbian and Gay Civil Rights, the Pennsylvania Log Cabin Republicans, OutFront, and the Pennsylvania Gender Rights Coalition.

Liberals have figured out how to stifle opposing views. It's a simple formula. Defend marriage and liberals call you a homophobe. Criticize someone like Al Sharpton or Jesse Jackson and liberals blast you as racist. They know the way to silence conservatives is to hurl names and accuse them of bigotry.

You know what? This tactic works. It's like being a victim of extortion or a frivolous lawsuit. Big companies sometimes settle rather than fight a nuisance lawsuit. They throw a handful of money at the pesky litigant to make the creep vanish. How can you blame them? Who wants to be called a bigot?

Rather than offend loony leftists, most people just keep their mouths shut, hoping the liberal activists quiet down. Trouble is, they never do. Our silence emboldens them. Come to think of it, maybe liberal activists interpret the majority's silence as agreement. Which makes it crucial to speak up, speak out, and express your feelings about issues like gay marriage. Write to elected officials, e-mail newspaper editors, call my show! Without our collective voices, it's only going to get worse. Maybe when the day comes that some freak is allowed to marry his cocker spaniel or a tree stump, people will stop worrying about offending the torchbearers of the liberal agenda.

I break ranks with many of my conservative colleagues and listeners when I say that gay marriage, although an issue to be tackled, is not the greatest threat to our nation's moral foundation. Heterosexuals need to get our own house in order before we fixate on gays and lesbians.

I often wonder how many of the men and women who rail against the gay agenda routinely cheat on their spouses. How many pastors who use their pulpits to preach against homosexuality have had an affair—or a series of illicit romps? Instead of focusing on gay marriage, we need to fix straight marriage.

In my early twenties, I became friends with a married man and his family. He was a great pal—funny, personable and likable. He had a beautiful wife who doted on him, a couple of terrific kids and a successful career. As I eventually learned, he also loved to have sex with other women. This secret devastated me. Why would this guy risk all he had for some sleazy woman he'd meet in a bar?

One day I asked him just that and our conversation has stuck with me all my life. "Mike, it's something I have to do. Just having sex with my wife is boring; I like to spice things up with some of these babes I meet on the side." When I asked him how he'd feel if his wife cheated on him, his double standard flashed like a neon sign. "I'd kill her," he said.

It's a mistake to believe that his behavior is an aberration. The skyrocketing divorce rate is proof that it is not. For many couples, their marriage is an annoyance, an obstacle to the pursuit of fun and excitement. And apparently it doesn't matter what your political beliefs are.

A few of my political heroes turned out to be less than stellar in their commitment to marriage, like Newt Gingrich, the former Speaker of the House of Representatives. His first wife told the *Washington Post* that Newt discussed divorce terms as she lay in a hospital bed, recuperating from cancer surgery. Divorce obtained, he then wed his younger girlfriend. Eighteen years later, he divorced wife number two after dallying with yet another younger woman, whom he also later married. Not good, Mr. Speaker. Rudy Giuliani stunned his supporters when he paraded around his girlfriend at the time, Judith Nathan, while his second wife and two children still lived in Gracie Mansion, the New York City mayor's official residence.

"Conservative" doesn't mean turning a blind eye to sins committed by our own torchbearers. I complained loud and long about how political icons like Newt and Rudy trampled on their marriage vows. In fairness, how could I do otherwise? It doesn't make sense to trash Bill Clinton for betraying his wife while isolating Republicans like Giuliani and Gingrich from similar criticism.

Regardless of our political views or party affiliation, we all should honor our marital vows and be faithful to our spouses. Why? Because marriage matters. It's the bedrock of our culture. We should treasure marriage by working hard at it every day of our lives.

Listen, I hate to sound holier-than-thou. Lord knows I'm not going to win any husband-of-the-year awards. I'm selfish, impatient and often cranky. But for me, my marriage to Denise *is* an ongoing celebration of fun and excitement. As I grew older (and grew up), I surrounded myself with friends who relish marriage, too, guys like Fieldin Culbreth.

Fieldin is a major league umpire who has become a good friend. As a former college baseball umpire, I've been able to meet a number of minor and major league umpires over the years. "Cubby," as Fieldin is known, has been in the big leagues since 1991 and is one of the classiest, happiest guys I know. Much of his joy comes from his wife and three children.

This is a guy who belongs to an elite group of professionals, who makes a good living, rubs elbows with superstars like the Yankees' captain, Derek Jeter, only travels first class and stays in the finest hotels. Yet, he is always saying how tough it is when spring training begins and he has to travel away from his wife, Claire, six-year-old-son, Fieldin IV, daughter Celina, age three, and baby daughter Shannon, one year old. During the season he does everything he can to get back to his home in South Carolina, a day here or a week there, to spend precious time with his family.

"It's the roughest part of what I do, leaving and going quite a few days without seeing them," he often tells me. "That's never easy, especially when they are young and growing. You miss an awful lot. If I didn't have to leave home, this would be the most perfect job in the world."

For Cubby, reaching the top of his profession is second to the beauty and joy of a loving wife and kids. All of the people I consider close friends give family the same high priority in their lives. People like John and Pam Dujardin, high school sweethearts after thirty-two years. Peter and Lisette Rief, my staff announcer and his wife who are still crazy about each other after twenty-six years. Burt and Linnae Young, a couple of successful career people who live for their next snorkeling vacation together. Bryant and Norma Quinn, who are as committed to each other as they are to their deep religious faith. Each of us men are fortunate to have met such wonderful partners.

I first saw Denise at a community theater production of *A Christmas Carol* in Greenville, South Carolina. I've always been an aspiring actor (probably with an ambition bigger than my talent). When I lived in Greenville, I starred in a number of plays and musicals there. You name a big role in musical theater, I've played it: Daddy Warbucks in *Annie*. Fagin in *Oliver*. The mad dentist in *Little Shop of Horrors*. Nicely-Nicely in *Guys and Dolls*.

In *A Christmas Carol* in 1990, I was cast as the Ghost of Christmas Present. A couple of seven-year-old twin boys played the role of Tiny Tim, alternating between performances. Their fifteen-year-old brother was in the show, too, playing a narrator and the goose boy. Their mother was my Denise.

Blond and gray-eyed, she caught my eye at one of the early meetings about rehearsal schedules and performance dates. I watched as she talked and laughed with everyone around her. She was beautiful but also confident, self-assured and attuned to others.

Denise flashes a warm smile and greets people when she walks into a room—not to make a splashy entrance but to make others comfortable by relating to every single person she meets. When I made my first clumsy attempt at talking to her about the play, she was warm and engaging. I was drawn to her from the first day I met her.

It was obvious from conversations I overheard that she was a single mom. Besides the three boys in the play (the twins Micah and Matthew and the oldest, Bryan), there was a fourth son at home, Trevor, then eleven years old. Despite the daunting prospect that I was becoming smitten with a lady who had four (gulp!) children, I forged ahead. This woman was special and I had to get to know her, definitely a priority after hearing that infectious laugh.

As rehearsals began, I began talking to her any chance I could, striking up conversations about everything from costume design to her boys' homework. I began offering to drive the kids home after rehearsals. Then, I started bringing dinner home with us. Before long, we had settled into a nice, comfortable routine. She was everything I thought—and more. She was the soul mate I never knew I desperately needed. I was in love.

But what about all those kids?

To begin with, the boys were—and are—incredible. They are four different kids with four different personalities: outgoing, sensitive Bryan; athletic, determined Trevor; upbeat, social Micah; and funny, loyal Matt. As their Mom and I began dating, it became apparent to me that they were great kids. They all seemed to accept me, even like me. No hurdles there. Denise and I grew closer and I knew that she was perfect for me. Denise seemed to think that I was the man for her. As great as everything was . . . what about all those kids?

Everyone in my life had an opinion. It was a pretty universal reaction, now that I think about it. A woman with four children? Don't walk away. Run. An instant family like that is a formula for disaster, everyone said. A single guy becoming the head of a six-person household? No way. Sure, Denise might be the one for you, but what about all those kids?

For many years now, I've had a mentor, a man who has influenced me as much as anyone in my life. Years ago, he taught me an important business and personal ethic: do the right thing. As basic as that sounds, I've found that life often throw us many chances to lie, or stretch the truth, or cut corners. This mentor is Greg Anderson, a guy whose name has come up a few times in this book. He was my general manager at the Greenville, South Carolina, radio station where I worked from 1989 to 1995. Years later we went our separate ways, me venturing into independent national syndication and Greg becoming the president of the Salem Radio Network. It was pure serendipity, a first in my life, when his company acquired *The Mike Gallagher Show*, allowing me to come full circle and work for this terrific man once more.

When I was struggling with how to move forward in my life with this wonderful woman and her children, it occurred to me. I should talk to Greg. He and his wife, Linda, enjoyed a solid, thriving marriage. He's a wise man and would undoubtedly give me sound advice. He did.

"If you love her, marry her," he said. "Don't pay attention to all the naysayers and second-guessers. You love her, you should marry her, and it will all fall into place."

It did. My marriage to Denise was the single best gift God has ever given me. The second was when I legally adopted the boys a few years after we were married. Our family is the most important thing in my life. Sure, there have been some setbacks as the kids went through all the typical adolescent and teenage debacles.

Some of the challenges were tough. Micah was diagnosed with

attention deficit disorder (ADD), which gives him creative juices making him a talented artist but can keep him incredibly hyper and unfocused. Trevor developed diabetes, and had to learn how to adapt his life to diet restrictions and insulin dependency. Micah and Trevor faced those problems with strength and courage. Like their brothers Bryan and Matt, they are loving, caring and selfless people. Their mother taught them well.

They had a role model in tackling life with grace and dignity. Denise put herself through college and became a paralegal in order to support them. I don't know, but maybe after I came into their lives they were also able to glean a thing or two from me. I just know that there is never a day that goes by that I don't thank God for letting us find each other.

Family is everything. A mother and father, raising their kids and squaring off against the world as a team, epitomize the quintessential American dream. Millions of us are blessed to be living it. Others aren't so lucky. When people say that family is the moral foundation of America, they're right. More than that, it's a blessing from God Himself.

Perhaps the reason that the divorce rate is so high is that many people dismiss marriage as expendable. Their focus is on what is convenient in their lives, or even easy. Marriage is anything but easy. And if a couple suffers from moral relativism and fails to acknowledge the sanctity of marriage, they're not likely to stay married very long.

"Family values" is a phrase that has lost its impact and meaning. Maybe it has been so overused that people have forgotten the essence of that phrase. We need to remind ourselves that family is more important than our work, our hobbies, or anything else. Nothing is as important as the joyful gift of a mother, father and their children.

The most important job any of us can ever hold is being a parent. As in marriage, I don't consider myself any kind of an expert. I don't have any degrees in family counseling. I'm not some radio shrink who dispenses advice, like Dr. Laura or Dr. Joy.

I'm just a guy who has loved being a dad. My entrance into the world of parenting came through adoption. We became a family, not through biological means, but due to a fierce and constant love. I have been incredibly lucky. Not one single time have any of the boys ever said to me, "You're not my dad." I am their dad. I've been their dad for years now. And I thank God that they know it, too.

I think it's fair to say that I learned my parenting skills on the fly. It was like a crash course. As the boys were growing up and we would be faced with one of their latest escapades, like one of them sneaking out of the house late at night, or getting a speeding ticket and not telling us, or one of them hosting a secret unsupervised party while Mom and Dad were out of town, I frequently wondered how I would ever survive it.

Somehow, we managed. Denise and I did our best to provide our kids a safe, loving place to grow up. We were strict but fair. And, naturally, Denise and I didn't always agree.

One of the early promises I made to myself was that as long as our children were living in our house, I was going to have the right to know everything they were doing. So I would routinely go through their rooms, even looking under mattresses and opening up drawers. I figured that if one of them was doing drugs or something similarly dangerous or illegal, I wanted to know about it right away so I could try to help them.

Denise believed that the boys should be allowed to have their privacy. Not a radical opinion, but one that I didn't share. Fortunately, she respected my position and my random room searches continued. I won't divulge any of the items that I found over the years out of respect to our sons, but let's just say that it was never anything too alarming.

I'm not sure that many people are committed to being the absolute best parents they can be. Parenting isn't a hobby or a part-time novelty. It's undoubtedly the most important responsibility we have. Nothing we do in life is as important. We're going to be leaving behind children who will teach their children who will teach their children and affect generations to come.

So why are so many parents so misguided in the way to do it?

One Sunday afternoon in New York City, Denise and I were outside one of our favorite restaurants. It was packed, so much so that a few of us had to wait outside on the sidewalk for a table. Joining us in the wait were a mother and father and their little son named Henry, who looked to be about seven or eight years old.

Mom and Dad were getting tired of waiting. "Henry," said the impatient and hungry mother. "We're going to go down the street to another restaurant. Mommy and Daddy are tired of waiting."

"*No!*" shrieked the little blond boy. "I wanna eat *here.*"

Denise and I gave each other a knowing smile. Surely this kid will get the inevitable lecture about being rude, his little hand will be grabbed and the three of them will go marching off to the restaurant down the street, just as the parents had wanted.

But we forgot that we're living in a different time now, an era where parents seem to want to be their child's friend, not their role model and authority figure. We failed to realize that many moms and dads have an entirely different approach these days.

It's called appeasement.

Henry's mom shot Dad a worried look. "C'mon, Henry, it'll be fun—we'll get you your macaroni and cheese that you like at the other place."

"*Nooooo!*" screeched the little brat. "*We are going to eat here!*"

By now, Denise and I were both thinking about what would be happening to that child if he were ours. As I've said before, we sure don't have all the answers to good parenting, but I sure as heck know that none of our children were going to bellow and carry on like that. Scratch that. If they'd acted like that, it would have been done only once. Either Denise or I would have given that child a good spanking, a stern lecture, and there is no doubt as to where the Gallaghers would have been eating that day.

But not Henry's parents. The dad began to take on a worried, pained expression. He had been down this road before.

"Hey, little man," Dad said. "If we can go to the other restaurant, we'll get you some ice cream afterward."

"*I said no!!!*" charming little Henry replied.

And that was that. Denise and I were seated and enjoying our brunch while Henry, Mom, and Dad kept standing outside. This seven-year-old child managed to lay down the law for his well-heeled, well-dressed, hungry and impatient parents. Little Henry wanted to eat at that place; they were going to eat at that place. That was all there was to it.

Over and over again, we see parents who seem imprisoned by their children's wishes. Somehow parents in 2005 are forgetting that they're the ones in charge, not the children. Maybe they think that constantly giving in to their kids will make life easier for everyone.

Such permissiveness will set that child up for a lifetime of disappointment and misery. Children want to be taught to do the right thing; they expect us to be in charge. Little Henry is going to grow into a person who figures that if he screams loudly enough, he'll always get his way. He'll develop into a person with an overwhelming sense of entitlement.

In other words, he'll become a liberal.

Liberals wallow in entitlement. Every single touchy-feely government handout program has been developed by liberal Democrats who believe that it's the government's role to make someone's life better.

Hearing from parents on my radio show all the time, there's a clear distinction between conservative parents and liberal ones. Conservatives believe in the power of spanking. A good swat on the behind goes a long way in reminding a child who's in charge. Liberals seem afraid to spank their children. They want to try and reason with them, to bribe them with ice cream, to understand their feelings and empathize with them. I'll bet anything that Henry's parents were a couple of liberal New York Democrats. Last time I checked they were still standing outside the restaurant, waiting to get in.

We live in a country that cherishes "family values." Getting married and raising a family is the real definition of the American dream. It doesn't matter how much money you make, how many cars you own, or how often you get to take a fancy vacation.

If you have family, you have everything you need. It's all that really matters.

# 10

# WHY DOES IT ALWAYS HAVE TO BE ABOUT RACE?

As a conservative with strong opinions against issues like affirmative action and slavery reparations, I sometimes get smeared with the "r" word: racist. That's the worst slur to a guy like me. Every time somebody calls me bigoted because I disagree with Jesse Jackson or the NAACP, it hurts.

On one radio show, I criticized former secretary of state Colin Powell for traveling to Mexico and embracing illegal immigration reform supported by the Mexican president, Vicente Fox. During that on-air discussion, a caller accused me of disliking Powell just because he's black. That's so hateful and untrue. I despise prejudice in all its forms.

When someone hurls the racist smear, I recall a sunny, summer day in 1992 in Greenville, South Carolina. I was enjoying a great life there as a local host and station manager at WFBC-AM. Dating Denise and advancing my radio career made the upstate of South Carolina beautiful to me. On that sunny afternoon, I took my beat-up 1984 Mercury Cougar for its annual inspection. The gas station attendant, a nice enough guy, said he'd be happy to inspect the car. The wait would just be a few minutes.

It was the end of the month, so a line formed. A minute or two later, a man drove up and asked the same attendant for an inspection. The guy cheerfully said, "Sorry, mister, we stopped inspecting cars a few minutes ago, we can't do anymore today."

That driver, a black man, saw the rest of us in the inspection line. A sad, knowing look flashed over his face. He nodded his head and walked slowly back to his car. It seemed odd to me that the station would stop inspecting cars so early in the afternoon. Moments after the black man drove away, another car arrived. The driver was white. "I need my car inspected," he said.

"No problem, buddy," said the attendant. "It'll just be a few minutes." The scene repeated when a second white driver appeared.

It finally hit me like a punch to the gut: the gas station attendant refused to inspect a black man's car. Now this ugliness wasn't over a job, or a college education or buying a home. It was a simple, meaningless gesture, proof that people can mindlessly hate. I was nauseated.

While slow to catch on, my reaction was quick. I told that gas station jerk that I didn't appreciate what he did. And I was forever taking my business elsewhere. His curses sounded like music to me as I drove off without the inspection.

Telling off the bigoted gas jockey and refusing to ever patronize his station was minuscule, I know, in the fight against racism. But I had to act. I will always remember the defeated look on that man's face when the gas station refused to serve him. He knew immediately what was happening; I was just a naïve bystander, unaccustomed to blatant displays of hatred.

Racism exists, flourishes in some places. You don't have to be a flaming liberal to understand that. As a conservative, I believe it's unfair to be attacked just because I might differ with liberals on how to fight racism or on the status of race relations in the United States in 2005.

For example, I believe we should be careful with words. The English language is a powerful force for furthering an agenda or reinforcing cultural ideals. The term "African American" annoys me. My parents were Irish and Lithuanian. Do you hear me calling myself an Irish American or Lithuanian American? Activists embraced African American as a reminder of black people's heritage. The ever-liberal, always politically correct news media and popular culture decided it was better to go along rather than risk offending the activists. So we're stuck with African American.

People who use that term don't even consider putting our own country first, as in American African. It's as if Africa remains the centerpiece of modern black American life. Sorry, I'd like to stick to "American," thank you very much. I'm an American, you're an American, we're all in this together—and none of us should care about skin color. If someone's race is relevant, let's refer to it openly. Not use some pseudo-intellectual, meaningless phrase like African American that only serves to polarize us.

Other racial phrases alarm me. Like the "N" word. Until the

O. J. Simpson trial, our country understood the evil behind the epithet "nigger." It was the word of lynching, of anguish, sadness and hate. It reverberated in practically every American household glued to coverage of the O. J. Simpson "Trial of the Century" in 1995. Los Angeles detective Mark Fuhrman was charged with perjury after testifying that he hadn't used the slur in a decade. (He later pleaded no contest to the perjury in a deal that spared him jail.) Audiotapes up to 1994 revealed that he had uttered the slur forty-one times while helping a screenwriter create a tough movie character. The defense capitalized on this to paint Fuhrman as a racist cop who would frame Simpson.

Hearing that slur again and again during the trial, some media type, probably someone at the *New York Times,* invented something called "the N Word." What a silly, sophomoric reaction. To pretend that the slur it stands for doesn't exist insults the millions of black Americans who suffered from all it means.

It also upsets me that the meaning of that slur has changed in some quarters. Flip on HBO, watch a Chris Rock special or listen to your local urban radio station. Young people and hip-hop artists call each other nigger and it's a positive, a term of endearment. Go figure.

All of us, white and black, must navigate current fashion, double standards, lack of personal responsibility, and political correctness in sifting through the complicated state of America's race relations. It's like walking through a landmine to criticize black politicians or stands taken by black organizations.

Like many conservatives, I am deeply critical of efforts to establish reparations for black Americans because of slavery. The rationale for reparations is ludicrous, that our country is supposed to hand over taxpayer dollars to blacks for what their ancestors may or may not have suffered by the ugliness of slavery. We're supposed to sit by while activists file lawsuits which would eventually result in all non-black Americans forking over our hard-earned money to black citizens.

Total, utter nonsense.

The issue of slavery reparations is like affirmative action a hundred times over, giving away something valuable regardless of merit or even need. If a white guy like me tries to complain, the knee-jerk reactionaries are ready to drop the "racist" bomb in a heartbeat.

It's not much easier for prominent blacks to criticize their own community. Comic legend Bill Cosby, one of America's favorite dads, lectured American blacks on being personally responsible for their actions, especially for supervising their children. Of course, he got flack for it. In the *New York Times* on May 22, 2004, Felicia R. Lee wrote about the incident:

> Bill Cosby, known mostly as a genial father figure who contributes to a wide range of black philanthropic causes, found himself immersed in controversy this week. After making inflammatory remarks on Monday about the behavior and values of some poor black people, Mr. Cosby said yesterday that he had made the comments out of concern and because of his belief that fighting racial injustice must also include accepting personal responsibility.
>
> Mr. Cosby spoke yesterday after a week of discussion on the Internet, on talk shows, on radio programs and in newspaper columns about his comments Monday night. . . . He has been attacked and applauded for saying that "the lower economic people are not holding up their end in this deal."
>
> He was also reported to have said: "These people are not parenting. They are buying things for their kids—$500 sneakers for

what? And won't spend $200 for 'Hooked on Phonics.' . . . They're standing on the corner and they can't speak English." . . .

Mr. Cosby's remarks, which also included the observation that not all incarcerated blacks are political prisoners ("people getting shot in the back of the head over a piece of pound cake, and then we run out and we are outraged") were meant to frame the complexities of black struggle. . . .

"I am in as much pain as many, many people about these people," he continued. "The 50 percent dropout rate, the seeming acceptance of having children and not making the father responsible and calling him in on it. It's easy to pass these things on like some kind of epidemic."

He said later in the conversation: "A 50 percent dropout rate in 2004 is not all about what people are doing to us. It's about what we are not doing. The Legal Defense Fund and the N.A.A.C.P. can deal on those points of law, but something has to come from the people." . . .

Makes sense, no? Instead of blacks blaming whites for society's transgressions, Dr. Cosby suggests that it's time for young Americans to take full responsibility for their actions. He's right. It's not the cop's fault that a young black man is in jail for shooting someone for a pair of expensive sneakers. It's not society's responsibility to ensure that blacks go to college or work hard to find respectable jobs and become productive members of society. The motivation must come from within.

Life throws obstacles at us all. Our responses define us.

As I mentioned, I lost my parents within ten years of each other, between the ages of eleven and twenty-one. Throughout that tumultuous decade, people constantly warned that I wasn't going to amount to anything in life. I was too much of a troublemaker in school and didn't apply myself to studies, they said. Despite their predictions, I walked into a radio station when I was a senior in high school, taking my first big step toward a respected broadcasting career.

Every American child will face setbacks and opportunities. Often, that child will have to dig deep to find the opportunities, but they exist. Blaming our country for its past sins is fruitless and only serves to keep those children from productive, creative, positive futures. Focusing less on race and more on individual merit is a good start on the long road to improving race relations.

# 11

# THANK YOU, JANET JACKSON

Who would have ever believed that Janet Jackson's breast could start a revolution?

By now, Ms. Jackson's "wardrobe malfunction" during the 2004 Super Bowl halftime show on CBS-TV has become notorious. As families gathered around the television set to watch one of America's grand traditions, they were treated to halftime "entertainment" that showed rap artists grabbing their crotches. The grand finale to this coarse display featured singer Justin Timberlake reaching out and ripping off a piece of Ms. Jackson's skin-tight costume, exposing her breast and "nipple jewelry."

Tivo, that wonderful invention that allows viewers to pause and replay live programming, reported an all-time record number of customers accessing that segment of the Super Bowl. What came next was extraordinary. Sure, there were the usual howls of protest and complaints about broadcast indecency. But this time, significant reforms loomed as a long-overdue crackdown on vulgar programming gathered steam. The Federal Communications Commission finally listened to the elected representatives of Congress who were listening to the American people. We had seen, and heard, enough.

For years, television and radio have been degenerating into a total cultural cesspool. TV shows like *Friends, Will and Grace, Coupling,* and *Desperate Housewives* ran on plotlines obsessively focused on sex: who would do it, when, with whom and how. Characters habitually slipped in double entendres and coy (and not so coy) references to the human anatomy. On radio, shock jocks turned their morning and afternoon drive shows into relentless marathons of striptease artists and porn stars. Their programs spewed filthy language and bathroom humor.

The FCC maintains specific guidelines prohibiting vulgar material over the free and public airwaves. Makes sense, right? The government licenses radio and television stations and expects them to refrain from airing indecent material. If not, the government can strip offending stations of their licenses and yank them off the air. The stakes are high. Successful radio and television stations rake in millions of dollars in revenues. Often, large publicly traded companies own these stations.

And so a ridiculous game ensues: let's pretend we don't *really* understand what "indecent" means. Yet in our hearts, we all do, even if some liberals won't admit it. As Supreme Court Justice Potter Stewart said in 1964 about hardcore pornography, "I shall not attempt further to define the kinds of material I understand to be embraced . . . but I know it when I see it."

After the Super Bowl scandal, the FCC decided to go after radio first. After all, what passes for material on many drive-time shows could be considered indecent not just by your grandmother, but by the average young person. Imagine what Justice Potter would have said, or done, about one radio show stunt I accidentally discovered while channel surfing in my car one afternoon.

I tuned into WNEW-FM's *Opie and Anthony*, then a ratings juggernaut in New York City. Those shock jocks had launched into their regular segment, "What's in Your Pants?" In this "comedy" bit, the duo encouraged young women to call the show and, while chatting live on the air, place the phone's handset down their dresses or pants. At the radio hosts' urging, the girls rubbed the phone against themselves. The snickering broadcasters then had to guess whether or not these women had shaved off their pubic hair.

This wasn't a one-time sophomoric stunt. It was a gimmick played regularly on *Opie and Anthony*. This show aired in New York City, the country's biggest, and presumably best, media market. Classy, eh? I dare any broadcast executive to keep a straight face while defending this kind of programming as "decent." Manage that feat and I say, give out the Academy Award.

Infinity Broadcasting's WNEW-FM radio ended up firing Opie and Anthony in the summer of 2002 for an even more infamous sex stunt. The shock jocks held a contest encouraging people to have sex in public places. One moronic couple from Virginia threw themselves into the effort. An usher saw them having sex inside the vestibule of St. Patrick's Cathedral, the soaring Gothic church that is the spiritual home for 2.4 million Catholics in the New York archdiocese.

The sex act happened shortly before 5 P.M. on a Thursday afternoon in August, as scores of tourists and worshippers filled the land-mark church. Hovering near the couple in the cathedral: an *Opie and Anthony* producer on his cell phone described the couple's tryst in a live broadcast to the shock jocks and their listeners. Police arrested the couple and the radio producer on public lewdness charges. The Catholic League filed a complaint with the FCC. The ensuing public outcry meant curtains for *Opie and Anthony.*

This show had crossed the proverbial line a long time before that stunt, as had many others. Shock jock Doug "Greaseman" Tracht made a racially insensitive comment that cost him his job at Washington's WARW in February 1999. After a song by the Grammy Award–winning Lauryn Hill, who is black, Tracht said, "No wonder people drag them behind cars." That was a reference to James Byrd Jr., the black man dragged to his death while tied to a pickup truck driven by three white men in Jasper, Texas.

Discussing the April 1999 massacre at Columbine High School, Howard Stern wondered why the teenaged gunmen didn't try to have sex with attractive girls at the school. Several stations tem-porarily yanked his show.

When singer Aaliyah died in a plane crash in August 2002, dee-jay Troi Torain, known as Star on New York's WQHT (HOT 97), played sounds of a screaming woman and a big crash. The station suspended him.

Even the 2004 tsunami in Southeast Asia, with its estimated death toll approaching 200,000 people, wasn't off-limits as joke ma-terial. Again HOT 97 found itself on the hot seat. Its morning crew played a parody called "The Tsunami Song," to the melody of "We Are the World," which used a slur for Asians and mocked their suffering. By late January 2005, the station suspended the morning talent amid calls by Asian groups to fire them.

Eventually, Opie and Anthony moved over to XM Satellite Radio, which is just where shock jocks belong. The advent of satellite radio companies like XM and Sirius is perfect for the millions of listeners who enjoy such broadcasters. If they can't do their jobs without resorting to indecent and obscene material, then listeners should have to pay for that titillation. Imagine how filthy they could get there. People should be able to hear them if they want to.

Howard Stern is the Lenny Bruce of our time. Many people find him funny while frequently profane, making Stern a multimillionaire. But Howard had a problem and it crashed down on him in the form of three letters: FCC.

The FCC began levying huge fines against radio stations that aired Howard's kind of programming. Somehow, this was turned into an attack on the First Amendment of the U.S. Constitution. "Free speech," the shock jock defenders proclaimed. "The government is now into censorship," they bellowed. What total nonsense.

Media giant Viacom must have realized the crackdown on indecency was here to stay. Viacom owns CBS-TV, plagued by the Janet Jackson striptease, as well as Infinity Broadcasting, whose radio stations aired Opie and Anthony and Howard Stern. In the largest settlement to date for FCC indecency fines, Viacom agreed to pay a record $3.5 million in November 2004. This amount covered three years' worth of violations, including the St. Patrick's Cathedral sex stunt. About $1.5 million of the total concerned complaints about Howard Stern.

"This consent decree allows us to move forward and to focus

our efforts in this area by serving our viewers and listeners with techniques to safeguard live broadcasts, such as cutaways and video and audio delays," Viacom said in a statement.

I've been a broadcaster for twenty-seven years. Since my first day on the job, I've known that I have a responsibility to avoid any content that could jeopardize my employer's license, not to mention an easy understanding of boundaries when it comes to morals and taste. Howard Stern doesn't own the airwaves or even the radio stations that broadcast him. No one has a right to expose people, particularly children, to indecent material over the free and public airwaves. Everyone understands that, right?

Evidently not.

Ever hear of *Girls Gone Wild?* Or gangsta rap? How about the latest escapade of the nation's favorite sitcom characters as they try to figure out which other character to sleep with, how often, and which bed to do it in? This overwhelming coarsening of our culture is a sad development recognized by all, although no one seems ready to try and change it. When Michael Powell stepped down as chairman of the Federal Communications Commission, a *New York Times* editorial ridiculed him for a "misguided" effort to restore decency to the free and public airwaves.

Once we wade through the filth of radio shock jocks and racy television content, we get to the saturation of violent video games that many of our kids relish. Perhaps this is all fueled by the liberal media's anything-goes, no-holds-barred permissiveness. But certainly, the line of decency has been crossed long ago. If adults want to purchase vulgar, indecent or obscene material, there's no shortage of suppliers. Shock jocks like Opie and Anthony or Howard Stern could play to their heart's content in the sandbox of satellite radio and make a fortune for that entity.

Listeners who need titillation on the radio with their morning coffee or afternoon drive home could hear their favorite jocks utter as many four-letter words as they take breaths. It just shouldn't be allowed on free and public airwaves.

This isn't censorship. It's regulation of broadcasters who have gone too far. And it's long overdue.

And we have Janet Jackson to thank for speeding up the reforms.

Thanks, Janet.

# 12

# FIELD OF BROKEN DREAMS

Pete Rose broke my heart.

Growing up in Dayton, Ohio, I idolized Pete "Charlie Hustle" Rose of the Cincinnati Reds. All of us kids who ran around in Dayton, just forty-five minutes from Cincinnati, loved the way Rose played ball. Scrappy, tough, ready to knock down any catcher in his way, Pete Rose was a baseball fan's delight.

He transformed his ordinary, fireplug of a body into a baseball machine. For twenty-four years in the majors, he epitomized toughness and perseverance. His 4,256 career hits remain the all-time highest total. Peter Edward Rose was simply an extraordinary baseball player. When he grew too old to play, he managed his beloved Reds. And ruined his career. Not on the field, but on the phone, placing bets.

Now those in professional baseball understand that gambling is the game's mortal sin. Abuse drugs, like the Yankees' Steve Howe or the Mets' Dwight Gooden or Darryl Strawberry and you'll get another chance. But gambling? Signs big as bulletin boards in the locker rooms of major league stadiums nationwide blare the warning of Rule #21:

> Any player, umpire, or club or league official or employee, who shall bet any sum whatsoever upon any baseball game in connection with which the bettor has a duty to perform shall be declared permanently ineligible.

Get the message? Gambling on baseball is forbidden.

In 225 pages of text and seven volumes of exhibits, a 1989 report by Major League Baseball's special counsel John Dowd accused Rose of gambling. The evidence in the report included betting slips, phone records, financial documents and testimony from witnesses.

While managing the Cincinnati Reds, Rose gambled like a fiend on the game he supposedly loved so much, said the report: "the accumulated testimony of witnesses, together with the documentary evidence and telephone records reveal extensive betting activity by Pete Rose in connection with professional baseball and, in particular, Cincinnati Reds games, during the 1985, 1986, and 1987 baseball seasons."

Rose denied that he bet on baseball, admitting only that he placed wagers on football and basketball games. In 1989, Commissioner of Baseball A. Bartlett Giamatti, former president of Yale University, banned Rose from baseball for life. Just like that, up in smoke went the lifetime of goodwill Rose had created among millions of fans like me.

Years ago, I was able to get a signed picture of Pete taken on his greatest baseball day. It showed him in 1985, the year before he retired, breaking Ty Cobb's milestone of 4,191 career hits. Rose cracked number 4,192 at Riverfront Stadium on Wednesday, September 11, 1985, a date I know well after staring at that picture in my office for years. In 2003, Rose published his autobiography, *My Prison Without Bars,* and made the media rounds in a sad attempt to rehabilitate his image. After almost twenty years of lying, Rose in this book supposedly came clean: he admitted gambling on baseball and on Reds games, but never against his own team.

That was it for me. I decided to protest his attempt to wheedle back into our good graces, probably aiming for a long-shot welcome back to baseball and admittance into the Hall of Fame. I took my treasured picture of Rose into the parking lot of my network radio studios in the Dallas area. Pouring gasoline on it, careful to stay away from the parked cars, I set the photo ablaze. A video camera recorded the entire scene.

Then on my Web site, Mikeonline.com, I posted the video for a fee, $4.98. All the proceeds would go to Gallagher's Army. It felt good to be able to raise money for the real heroes by burning a photo of the guy who had once been my sports hero but turned into such a creep.

Pete Rose is just one example, albeit extreme, of sports stars who forfeit the trust and admiration of legions of fans to indulge in some sordid, illegal and ultimately selfish act. It seems we constantly hear about famous athletes who take for granted their gift and its attendant fame and riches.

Take Tiger Woods. Young, handsome, and charismatic, the superstar golfer is the quintessential American success story. He'll go down in history as one of golf's all-time greats. Tiger has inspired millions of young people, black and white, to strive for greatness.

So what's with his penchant for cursing? Here's a guy who can concentrate like a mind reader, who can calmly sink a fifteen-foot putt while the world watches. Yet he lacks the self-control to stop using the vilest swear words during tournaments.

One Saturday afternoon, as "Tiger Woods hype" was in full bloom, his pictures on tons of magazine covers, I watched him play in a tournament. Like everyone else, I was rooting for this golfing sensation. As he neared the third or fourth green, he hit a chip shot. The camera zoomed in on his face just in time to catch him mouth the words, "God D—it." A few holes later, same routine: a bad shot, close-up of Tiger, and this time it was "F— me."

Some role model.

Let me get this straight: the guy is a genius at the game of golf, savvy enough to negotiate multimillion-dollar endorsement deals, and he can't stop cussing like a street thug as fifteen cameras and millions of fans watch his every move?

No way. He could stop. Tiger Woods wants to keep swearing. He doesn't care about the responsibility he has to a world full of young, impressionable fans who will emulate him.

Charles Barkley, the retired NBA star forward, made headlines in 1991 insisting that he's *not* a role model, that kids and parents make a huge mistake in putting professional sports stars on pedestals. "I don't think because I can dunk a basketball they should want me to be a role model," Barkley said. "I know drug dealers who can dunk the basketball.

"Some athletes are perfect, perfect role models, but they're not good guys behind the scenes. Then you've got guys who are portrayed negative because maybe they get to fighting every now and then or they're holding out contracts or get into it with the media, and they may be great guys. So, that's why you don't want athletes to be role models, because a lot of phony stuff goes around."

He's probably right, to some degree. After all, we don't really know the character of the rare person who can shoot a basketball or field a baseball or hit a golf ball well enough to earn millions of dollars.

Don't fool yourself, though, or let Charles Barkley kid you, either. Professional sports stars dream of the spotlight long before it shines on them. Ask any major league baseball player and he'll admit how he practiced his autograph years before he even began playing in the minor leagues.

These athletes choose to walk in the klieg lights of professional sports. Like it or not, that decision brings added responsibilities for their public image and its influence over fans, particularly young ones. Kids collect a star's trading cards, ask for autographs and pretend to be their hero in their dreams.

So with the development of so many young minds at stake, can it really be that difficult for Tiger Woods to bite his tongue?

Other sports stars need to control their fists. In the fall of 2004, back-to-back rumbles showed how volatile and even violent athletes can be. One happened with the Tigers of Clemson, the team I used to cover on the tailgate show and as the sideline reporter.

At the annual Clemson/South Carolina football game on Saturday, November 20, 2004, a huge brawl erupted between the teams. There were just 5:48 minutes left in the game. Clemson dominated, winning 29–7. From the melee came one of the ugliest and widely published pictures of the year: a helmeted Clemson player kicking a South Carolina player who was facedown on the turf, minus his helmet.

A promising result from that vicious, awful day in Clemson, South Carolina, was that the schools punished themselves by forgoing any bowl games. Both teams would have been eligible but they stayed benched for the holidays. "Attending a bowl game is important to the Clemson family, but nothing is more important than the integrity of the university," said school president James F. Barker. This was a good lesson for college athletes who had broken all the rules of sportsmanship.

Less than twenty-four hours before that gridiron fight, the infamous NBA "basket-brawl" exploded between five Indiana Pacers and several Detroit Piston fans at the Palace of Auburn Hills, Michigan, November 19, 2004. Watching NBA star Ron Artest in a full-fledged fistfight with people in the seats was so traumatic for witnesses, they actually broke down and cried, including a terrified little boy, who was widely photographed.

Artest was suspended for the rest of the NBA season, a history-making punishment. The Oakland County, Michigan, prosecutor charged Artest and four other Pacers with misdemeanor assault. Seven fans were also collared.

It could be argued that the fans who threw beer, a chair and other objects at the players were equally to blame. Once again, it was Charles Barkley with some words of wisdom, saying, "I'm not saying Ron Artest was right for going into the stands. But we are not animals in a zoo, because we make a lot of money, you can throw things at us. Anybody who thinks that is stupid."

Ultimately, nothing can wipe away the disgraceful images of a street fight between professional basketball players and fans. We've seen that plenty of college and professional athletes sorely lack class. They should take a lesson from a star that is worlds away from that bad behavior.

Like Emmitt Smith.

Our twenty-two-year-old son Matt is a Dallas Cowboys fan. Scratch that, he's a Dallas Cowboys fanatic. The single most appreciated gift my wife Denise and I have ever given him was his Cowboys season ticket when we scored four of them in a prime spot at Texas Stadium, about nine rows from the field and near the forty-yard line.

Matt lines his bedroom walls with Cowboys posters, his shelves with team memorabilia. He idolizes former Cowboy Emmitt Smith, the legendary running back, one of the greatest to ever play the game. After fifteen years in the NFL, Smith had a spectacular season in 2004. As a thirty-five-year-old with the Arizona Cardinals, Smith became the league's career rushing leader, the first player to ever surpass the 18,000-yard milestone. He recently announced his retirement and is a shoo-in for the Hall of Fame.

Off the field, Smith is known as a dignified, gracious, religious family man who never takes his athletic gift for granted. At age twenty-five, he started Emmitt Smith Charities Inc., raising millions over the years for hungry children, inner-city youths and other deserving groups.

What a joy to personally discover just how authentic his reputation really is. It happened during Emmitt Smith's last year with the Cowboys. It was off-season in the spring of 2003. Matt was on a plane to Philadelphia, visiting his girlfriend, Marisa, who attended Villanova University. While dozing in the back of the coach section, he heard someone say that "some football player" was up in first class. "Emmitt somebody-or-other."

Could it be true? Could Matt's hero, the single greatest running back in football history and star of his beloved Cowboys, actually be on the plane? Matt leaned over and peered down the long plane aisle and saw a shaved head, Emmitt's trademark style. When the plane landed, Matt sprinted past rows of passengers to confirm the sighting. With his backpack flapping and shoes flopping, Matt ran down the escalator to see Emmitt Smith in baggage claim, waiting like everyone else. Well, he wasn't exactly like everyone else; he was the only passenger with a burly bodyguard.

Matt had never been so excited and nervous. Finally, a chance to meet the star he had spent years admiring. He approached the football great. Smith's bodyguard immediately stepped between them, saying "I'm sorry, kid, but Mr. Smith isn't able to sign autographs today."

Matt Gallagher, our once shy and quiet son, persevered. "Please, sir," he said. "I don't want his autograph. I just want to be able to shake his hand and tell him how much he means to me."

The bodyguard shook his head no and stood his ground. But Number 22 himself put his hand on his bodyguard's shoulder and gently pushed him aside. "It's okay," he said.

With that simple gesture, my son was given a moment that he never thought possible, one that he will cherish his whole life. He shook Emmitt's hand and thanked him for being such a great inspiration to him, both on and off the field. Smith just beamed and graciously thanked him.

You never hear of Emmitt Smith cursing in front of the TV cameras. He's not betting on football games, doing drugs, beating his wife or cheating on his taxes. Confronted with an eager fan in a crowded airport in Philadelphia, he took a minute to give that young man, our son Matt, a lifelong memory. I will be forever grateful.

Instead of breaking hearts, a professional athlete like Emmitt Smith is capable of filling a young fan's heart with joy. That's a true star.

Pete Rose and Tiger Woods can learn a thing or two from him.

# 13

# THE HOLLYWOOD BUNCH

Who doesn't like watching famous people? Star-gazing is an American pastime.

At age fifteen, I practically stalked a Dayton TV sportscaster, Omar Williams. I was so excited about seeing him at the mall that I started tailing him in and out of the stores, marveling at my luck in spotting "the Dean of Dayton TV Sports" in Sears. Years later, when I worked at Omar's station, Channel 2 in Dayton, it was still hard for me to believe that I had become his backup sports anchor. When I confessed to Omar that I had stalked him in the mall long ago, he looked uneasy and quickly changed the subject.

Omar and I became friends, which helped control my hero worship of the guy. My awe fades when I actually befriend famous or accomplished people, like Omar, or actress Sally Struthers, Gloria in

the '70s hit *All in the Family.* It's because I get to know the people behind the names. When I like and admire them as friends, I stop staring at them as if they're rare paintings.

Sally Struthers is an amazing woman. Despite being a beloved
TV icon, she's managed to raise a beautiful, thoughtful daughter and
is to this day able to extend kindness and graciousness to everyone
she meets. As my wife frequently puts it, Sally has an aura about her,
a kindness that just oozes from her pores.

Our fascination with celebrity fuels the runaway phenomenon
that is Reality TV. Many Americans apparently dream of the spotlight, or at least tune in by the millions to see how fame affects regular folks. There's also the notoriety factor, which is why I'm now
addicted to *Growing Up Gotti.* This reality feast showcases blond, be-
jeweled Victoria Gotti, daughter of the late mob boss John Gotti,
and her three macho, hair-gelled sons.

Despite America's love of star-gazing, however, I cannot fathom
why *anyone* cares about an actor's opinion of our president or the war
on terror. While I'm happy to spot a famous face, I don't care about
that face's politics. If those views differ greatly from my own, I begin
disliking that star. Immensely. Many people share my feelings. I'm
sure that Barbra Streisand's left-wing ideology and Whoopi Goldberg's crass attacks on George W. Bush have lost them many fans.

The Hollywood crowd is a beautiful, privileged bunch, blessed
with God-given gifts. Most are physically stunning. They possess
some artistic talent—they can sing, or act, or dance, or even just pose
for the camera and smile prettily. Their talents have brought them
riches and conveniences like private jets and live-in maids. Theirs is a
life of privilege and wealth, which is all well and good, the American
dream.

Until they open up their big mouths, revealing a gigantic arrogance and sense of entitlement. Take Ed Asner, for instance.

"You saw what we did to Rush Limbaugh, didn't you?" hissed the actor, known forever as Lou Grant from his stint on *The Mary Tyler Moore Show.*

"Well, Hannity is next," he warned.

I found myself hearing "Mr. Grant" hint of a left-wing plot against my friend, Sean Hannity, because I was indulging in my adolescent penchant for star-gazing. I was at a "junket."

This junket, or press event, was for a new movie. Usually I'm invited to these events when a studio wants me to see a new film that will be advertised on my radio show. Studio junkets are lavish. Guests stay in five-star hotels, hobnob with the famous, attend a private film screening, eat generously on the studio's dime and receive a basket filled with expensive gifts. Me, I just like the chance to meet the stars.

The release of the Christmas movie *Elf,* starring comic Will Ferrell, brought me a junket invitation. The gala in Manhattan transformed the luxurious Regency Hotel into a Christmas extravaganza in October, filling the lobby with holiday decorations and Christmas trees. The highlight was a cocktail party, high atop the Empire State Building, with the *Elf* stars: Ferrell, Bob Newhart and Ed Asner. It was a blast.

Asner is a radical liberal. So when we met, I thought it fair to warn him who I was, that I wasn't an entertainment reporter or movie reviewer. My radio career seemed to grab Asner's attention. The news had just broken about Rush Limbaugh's addiction to prescription painkillers. Most of us in talk radio are fiercely loyal to Rush. As I've mentioned, his groundbreaking success allowed us to carve out wonderful careers.

So here I am telling Ed Asner I work in the same business as conservative giants like Rush and Sean Hannity. Then he lobbed his venom on Rush and Sean. It took a few seconds for his words to sink in. Was he taking credit, on behalf of liberals everywhere, for Rush's misfortune? And what about this kooky threat about Sean's fate?

When he said, "Hannity is next" to me, I was practically speechless. I said, "Well, I'm sure sorry you feel that way," then I just turned around and walked away, leaving him standing there, smirking at me. I wasn't going to spend another iota of time or energy with a creep like him. This is a perfect example of the kind of personal and visceral contempt Hollywood liberals like Ed Asner have for decent people like Rush and Sean and all the rest of us.

Let's say instead of Rush, a prescription drug scandal ensnared a gangsta rapper who made millions bragging about killing police officers or beating his wife. Leftists like Asner would line up to defend him. After all, he is among those ultraleftists, like Angela Davis and actress Susan Sarandon, so out of touch with reality they advocate "justice" for black activist Mumia Abu-Jamal, a dreadful cop-killer.

In 1981, Abu-Jamal, a part-time radio reporter and cab driver, mercilessly gunned down twenty-five-year-old Philadelphia police officer Daniel Faulkner. Faulkner had pulled over a car driven by Abu-Jamal's brother. Prosecutors charged that Abu-Jamal ran over to the cop and shot him in the back, face and chest. His widow, Maureen, has endured more than twenty years of second-guessing from the leftist fringe who insist a racist court system convicted Abu-Jamal. Rubbish.

She suffered a major setback in 2001, the twentieth anniversary of her husband's execution, when a federal appeals judge upheld Abu-Jamal's conviction but threw out his death sentence. This came on the heels of another outrage: the city council of Paris made Abu-Jamal an honorary citizen of France's capital. Two years later, the socialist mayor of Paris also honored the convicted killer.

"As for making this man an honorary citizen," Maureen Faulkner told Bill O'Reilly in 2003, "they talk about capital punishment, they talk about the death penalty and the barbarity of it all. Well, what about the barbaric act Mumia Abu-Jamal made when he shot my husband in the back and when my husband fell to the ground, he stood over him and emptied his gun into his face, shooting him?"

Asner's politics are so pitifully skewed. When a conservative American icon like Limbaugh is suffering from drug addiction, Asner is gleeful. A guy like Asner believes that the world cares about his far-out views on social or political issues. Challenge one of these Hollywood elitists and they howl like a caged animal.

To celebrate the anniversary of a great baseball movie, *Bull Durham,* the Baseball Hall of Fame in Cooperstown planned to throw a big party. The Hall of Fame was an appropriate venue to celebrate such a terrific film about America's pastime. The film's outspoken and controversial liberal stars, Tim Robbins and Susan Sarandon had been invited—until their antiwar comments caused the Hall of Fame to cancel the event.

On April 9, 2003, Ben Walker reported for the Associated Press that "Hall president Dale Petroskey sent a letter to Robbins and Sarandon this week, saying the festivities April 26–27 at Cooperstown, N.Y., had been called off because of their remarks. Petroskey, a former White House assistant press secretary under Ronald Reagan, said recent comments by the actors "ultimately could put our troops in even more danger."

Robbins, of course, couldn't understand this logic. Walker continues, "Reached Wednesday night, Robbins said he was 'dismayed' by the decision." He responded with a letter he planned to send to Petroskey, telling him: "You belong with the cowards and ideologues in a hall of infamy and shame." . . .

Classy, eh?

If the folks running the Hall of Fame are uncomfortable with featuring a couple of well-known liberal activists like Tim Robbins and Susan Sarandon, that is entirely their prerogative. Who in the world stomps their feet and throws a temper tantrum when they're kept from a party, other than five-year-old children and pampered movie stars?

Want to watch Hollywood liberals go bonkers? Dare to suggest that the world doesn't owe them a living. Take comic Whoppi Goldberg. She had a gig pitching the Slim-Fast diet regime. In TV ads, she proclaimed herself a "big loser" for shedding pounds.

Well, Goldberg lost, all right—she lost this lucrative job. Slim-Fast dumped her for mocking President Bush in a sexually tinged rant playing on his surname. The presidential candidate John Kerry watched her distinguish herself in this manner on the stage of Manhattan's historic Radio City Music Hall at a Democratic rally that raised $7.5 million in July 2004, laughing at all the punch lines and clapping enthusiastically during the dirty jokes at the expense of our commander in chief.

No wonder he got clobbered in the 2004 election.

"We are disappointed by the manner in which Ms. Goldberg chose to express herself and sincerely regret that her recent remarks offended some of our consumers," said Slim-Fast. "Ads featuring Ms. Goldberg will no longer be on the air."

Goldberg cloaked herself in the First Amendment: "The fact that I am no longer the spokesman for Slim-Fast makes me sad, but not as sad as someone trying to punish me for exercising my right as an American to speak my mind in any forum that I choose."

She doesn't get it. It's not about free speech. She enjoys that right, like all Americans. Equally, Slim-Fast has the right to decide that Goldberg's free speech offends millions of people; as a company they have a right to run from her because of that vile routine. After all, she is a spokesperson for the company, and like any business they want to attract customers, not drive them away. They dumped her—in a skinny minute.

Ditto for *Lethal Weapon* star Danny Glover. He had been the spokesman for MCI, the telecommunications giant. That was before he blasted President Bush, criticized the Iraq war and signed a letter supporting Cuban dictator Fidel Castro that suggested America would invade the communist island.

Angry letters, phone calls and e-mails flooded into MCI from irate customers who didn't want this guy to be their spokesman. MCI fired him. Some portrayed Glover as the victim of forces "oppressing free speech." There was nothing free about his arrangement with MCI. They paid, he spoke. He read lines from a script that MCI provided. If he is the face of a company, he should be careful about what he says.

MCI has every right to hire or fire at will. Hollywood elitists who object when a business decides to dump loud-mouthed liberals, like Goldberg and Glover, reveal their delusional sense of entitlement.

None of us who make money in any occupation are guaranteed a career, except, perhaps, pampered college professors with tenure or judges who receive lifetime appointments. Still, Hollywood blowhards who use their celebrity to voice shrill, anti-American positions seem to think that they can say anything without facing consequences.

Sorry, folks, America doesn't work that way. Do your job, pay your taxes, and stay out of trouble. If you express strong opinions, be prepared to take the heat.

Only radio talk show hosts are allowed to spout off with impunity.

# 14

# FIGHTING FAT— ANOTHER WAR WORTH WINNING

"Mike, I'm so excited about you writing your first book," said the cheerful, plump lady who shook my hand at a listener "meet and greet" party in Decatur, Illinois. "Now whatever you do, make sure you write about how you lost all that weight. That's something that *everyone* can relate to." She's right.

Obesity is America's huge health crisis. It's so rampant that bad diets and physical inactivity are poised to surpass tobacco as the country's leading preventable cause of death, according to the federal Centers for Disease Control. It's also becoming fashionable to blame everyone and everything except for the person stuffing the food in his or her mouth for being fat. Blaming the Big Mac for someone's obesity is a hallmark of loony liberalism. It's a complete abdication of personal responsibility. Like the klutzy lady who sued McDonald's because she spilled a cup of hot coffee in her lap, the screwballs who have filed lawsuits against the fast food industry for their ever-expanding girth are proof-positive that there are plenty of people who can't take responsibility for their own behavior.

But try as I might, I cannot find a valid reason to blame liberals for all the years I've been fat. It's tempting, but wrong, to blame my parents: working-class Catholic Democrats who never counted a carb. They lived in a different era and died when I was pretty young. My dad lost his fight with leukemia on Christmas Day 1971 when I was eleven; bladder cancer claimed my mom a decade later, also at Christmastime. The timing of their deaths might explain why I often used the holidays to gorge myself.

After my dad died, my mom and I started an odd but endearing Christmas Eve tradition. We would go to the McDonald's on Salem Avenue in my hometown of Dayton, Ohio, and have a pre-Christmas meal: I'd order two Big Macs, fries and a Coke. Now this was a blast for a twelve- or thirteen-year-old kid on Christmas Eve, but c'mon, Mom, *two* Big Macs? As Dr. Phil would say today: What were you thinking, Marge? But I absolve my mom for those Big Macs. I ate them and loved every minute of it. And as I got older, it wasn't my mom stuffing food into my face, but me.

Some fatties think that they're overweight strictly because of cultural, genetic, or even economic factors. Of course, there's always the rare exception, as with the story of Anamarie Martinez-Regino of Albuquerque, New Mexico, who weighed ninety pounds at age three and a half. State authorities suspected her family was overfeeding the girl. In late August of 2000, the state took the girl from her home, placing her in foster care. Her parents insisted that they watched her diet and blamed her weight on a medical condition that doctors have yet to diagnose. A few months later, she was returned home.

In a follow-up, *Good Morning America* visited the girl and her family in the summer of 2004. Anamarie was still growing at an abnormally fast rate—weighing 180 pounds and standing five feet one as a seven-year-old about to enter second grade. Her mother insisted she carefully watches the 1,200 calories a day she feeds the girl.

This is clearly a highly unusual case. Otherwise, the great majority of the blame for those who are fat lies with those who are fat. The sooner people own up to their personal responsibility to eat less, the healthier we'll be and the longer we'll live. And I'm not talking about a minority of the population—about two-thirds of American adults are overweight. Two-thirds! And about half of those people are obese. The problem is even worse in black and Latino communities. The U.S. surgeon general says we're spending about $117 billion a year on fat-related problems and diseases—and that amount is growing.

Few accomplishments in my life are as personally satisfying as losing seventy pounds and keeping them off. I'm so proud that I finally woke up and realized that it was all up to me, that I had to stop being lazy and complacent, enjoying a smorgasbord of cheeseburgers, fried chicken, fatty casseroles, french fries and chocolate chip cookies. If I slipped up and mixed in a salad, it was drenched in chunky blue cheese dressing. You get the picture.

As my career started growing, so did my waistline. The more

time I spent on the road, the easier it became to shove fast food in my mouth. When I moved to New York City in 1996, I was pushing 230 pounds. By the end of 2001, I topped 255 pounds. Not a pretty picture for a guy who's a little over five feet eleven.

Before Fox News Channel hired me exclusively, I also appeared on other cable news networks, like CNN, Court TV, and CNBC and MSNBC. Toward the end of his ill-fated MSNBC show, Phil Donahue liked using me as one of his show's token conservatives. One of the nicest and most gracious broadcasters I've ever met, Phil always treated me with kindness and respect despite our ideological differences. It was neat to appear on his show since he became a national television star in my hometown of Dayton. It was there, in the studios of WLWD-TV, that his talk show was launched and syndicated nationally before he moved it to Chicago.

When I was bouncing between cable shows, we were living full-time in Dallas. To appear on *Donahue,* the show's producers flew me into New York. On this particular occasion it was a cold, rainy January night in 2002. While in the green room at 30 Rockefeller Center prior to the show, I met another righty, Joel Mowbray, a writer and solid conservative voice in America. Like most green rooms, where guests wait, Donahue's had platters of food and beverages. I watched Joel make some ham and cheese sandwiches, twisting them into long wraps without any bread.

"Another Atkins guy, eh?" I said to him.

"You'd better believe it," he answered. "It was fairly quick and painless, I lost eighty pounds, and I've kept it off for four years now."

Four years. His words hit me like a splash of ice water. Why couldn't I do that, too? I was feeling fat and sloppy and I just couldn't stand it. Looking at Joel, I thought, Can it really be as easy as he says?

Then it was showtime. On the set for our segment, I blotted out our conversation. I remember even stuffing potato chips and onion dip in my mouth before I took the car service back to the hotel. Motivation for slimming down would have to wait.

Back at the hotel, I was miserable. I hate traveling without Denise. It was one of those bitter, nasty winter nights in Manhattan. Whoever called crowded New York the world's loneliest city knew the score. I couldn't sleep and began channel surfing. I came upon MSNBC and a rebroadcast of the Donahue show I had appeared on earlier that evening.

Wow, was I disgusting.

There I was, in all my fatness. I couldn't pay attention to the conversation, my appearance so repulsed me. Big, flabby jowls hung over a dress shirt that threatened to strangle the life out of my huge neck. I looked awful. Sort of like Jabba the Hut in a button-down shirt.

Alone in that hotel room, watching my immense size fill the TV screen, motivation hit. I was going to lose weight. As God is my witness, I was going to lose weight. I got on my knees at the side of the bed and prayed to God for the strength to keep my vow. Then I called home and woke up Denise.

"I've had it," I screamed at her. I think she was convinced I had lost my mind, a regular event in our marriage.

"No more being fat for me. This guy told me tonight how easy Atkins would be, and I'm starting tomorrow. *No More Carbs!*"

To my diet-cheating heart, the beauty of the Atkins diet was the tons of red meat, all the cheese and eggs and bacon I could eat, and pour on that blue cheese. I was going to be in hog heaven! I started Atkins the next day. I didn't follow any specific plan. I just eliminated carbohydrates. Sure enough, I dropped twenty pounds in about three weeks. Those results amazed me. But it was not—allow this cliché, please—all a piece of cake for me. I craved those breads and pastas. I longed for a Diet Pepsi or Diet Coke, also forbidden.

When Denise, the kids and I went out to eat one night and I tried to eat a cheeseburger without the bun, I gagged. Ever try eating a Whopper with cheese from Burger King without the bun? Don't, I warn you. It tastes terrible. Since I hadn't read an Atkins book or followed specific, healthy guidelines I began to realize flying blind wasn't working. I couldn't piece together a coherent nutritional plan day to day and I was beginning to feel aimless. It was time for the action I've taken so many times in my pathetic life: turn to my wife.

Denise has always believed in Weight Watchers. Unlike me, she takes the time to read, study and evaluate. She introduced me to their points system, where every food counts for a number of points. She agreed to go on the plan with me and we even went to meetings together, a huge concession by me, since I had always vowed to never attend a fatty confession fest. Armed with a healthy, sensible plan this time, I dived in headfirst. Boy, did it work.

I'd lose five pounds one week, maybe two or three the next. Heck, there were some weeks I didn't lose anything. But slowly and surely, I was losing the weight. I saw it in my face, I felt it in my loosening clothes, and I watched it on the scales for my weekly weigh-ins.

It took a little over a year, but I went from 255 pounds to the 185 pounds I weigh today.

What's the secret? There is none. Simply staying faithful to a steady routine that I developed worked well for me. It doesn't matter which specific plan you choose. Weight Watchers, Atkins, the Zone Diet, South Beach, Makers Diet—they've all been proven successful. Losing weight starts with an ironclad commitment to changing your life. We all fear hunger. "I can't possibly get though the afternoon hunger pangs," we moan. "I'm gonna go crazy if I can't have a bunch of chips or a few cookies before that big meeting later today."

That's total nonsense. I'm convinced that the unreasonable fear of hunger is what drives so many of us into sizes only carried by big- and tall-persons' stores (I used to call it "the Fat Man's Store"; Denise, ever sympathetic, called it "the Fluffy Man's Store"). So what if you have a few hunger pangs at some point in the day? Trust me, you're not going to wither up and die. Drink a glass of water, pop a few grapes. Stay busy. It'll pass.

I hate the phrase, "going on a diet." To me, that's like signing a prenuptial agreement. You've already convinced yourself that you're going to fail before you even start. Losing weight and keeping it off isn't "going on a diet." It's changing the way you eat, every meal, every day.

People often ask me how I did it. Losing seventy pounds is fairly dramatic. I'll share the routine that let me drop six inches from my waist size. It's the day-to-day routine I follow that has me in a medium-sized golf shirt after wearing an XXL.

As I list my guidelines, keep in mind that losing weight was one of the easiest, most painless accomplishments of my life. I promise, it can be for you, too. Of course, I'm not a doctor, so you should consult with one before beginning any diet and exercise regimen.

For me, reducing mealtime portions was key and simple. I followed the Weight Watchers points system, but any method of reducing meal and snack portions will work wonders. It's all about limiting those portions.

## MIKE'S DAILY MEAL ROUTINE

**Breakfast** Eggs, cereal, or oatmeal. Usually 6 to 7 points.

**Lunch** A Weight Watchers meal popped into the office microwave. Anywhere from 4 to 6 points.

**Late afternoon snack** A small bag of pretzels or a low-fat cookie. Usually 3 to 4 points.

**Dinner** Wide open, as long as it doesn't exceed around 12 or 13 points. For example, baked ziti is a great Italian meal that doesn't have a ton of points. Two cups of ziti is around 12 points.

**Late night snack** A Weight Watchers Fudge Bar (truly heaven on earth). One point.

That routine worked. And it let me keep the weight off. After a time, there are few, if any, hunger pangs. I've noticed that as I fell into the pattern of eating smaller portions, I really stopped wanting to overeat. I don't know if the old saying that the less you eat the smaller your stomach becomes is true, but it does feel that way. I can tell you, though, that if you eat smaller portions five or six times a day, you'll feel a lot more satisfied than eating two or three huge meals a day.

Here are my unbreakable guidelines:

★ Drink lots of water. I usually try to drink between two and three twenty-ounce sports bottles of water per day.

★ Do around thirty minutes of some kind of exercise daily. Anything works for me—a daily walk, thirty minutes on a treadmill, even thirty minutes of fairly intense laps in the pool.

★ Get support from a loved one or good friend. You really need a partner in this. Like life, it's hard to go it alone. If you falter, draw on encouraging words from them. If they stumble, urge them on. You'll receive strength from each other.

★ Keep an old picture of yourself as a fatty in a spot you'll see daily. My fat picture stays on my desk. It's an amazing motivator.

The weight crisis is hitting children particularly hard. America's kids are fat and getting fatter. One in six children between the ages of six and nineteen are fat. Another 15 percent are close. That means that nearly one in three children is either overweight or dangerously close to being so.

We often discuss the need for parents to do their jobs and do the right thing by our children. After all, we're all they've got. Just like my mom probably meant well by watching her son devour two Big Macs at a time ("Go ahead and eat, Mikey, you're a growing boy!"), today's parents think they're somehow helping their children by force-feeding them into fathood.

Not long ago at an airport, I saw an awful example of this misguided parenting. People-watching is great theater and there is no better stage than an airport while you are waiting for a flight. I became engrossed in watching a young mother and her little boy. "Charlie," as I'll call him, was probably around nine or ten years old. Mom was an attractive, doting lady who seemed intent on feeding her already-chubby child. I'll re-create the conversation I overheard in this actual event that I witnessed with my own eyes and ears.

MOM: Charlie, are you hungry? We're gonna get on the plane in about forty-five minutes, you wanna eat?

CHARLIE: Naw, Mom, I'm okay.

MOM: Charlie, you need to eat. You know how you get if you're hungry, you'll be a grumpy gus.

CHARLIE: I'm not hungry!

MOM: You hafta eat, Charlie, and that's that. What do you want from Burger King?

CHARLIE: Awww, Mom, I don't want *anything* from Burger King.

MOM: Charles, you don't allow me to get you some food, you
will be in *big* trouble, mister. Now what do you want?

At this point, I wanted to jump up and start screaming at this
annoying dimwit of a mother. The little pudgy boy didn't *want*
Burger King, didn't *want* to have to eat, he was doing just fine playing with his Gameboy. But Mom was simply not going to back
down.

MOM: I am going down to Burger King and get you something
to snack on—you wait right here, do not move.

Naturally, I'm tempted to grab the kid and run for the nearest
exit, trying to save him from a life of misery with this overbearing,
Joan Crawford of a mother. But I think they have laws against that
sort of thing. . . . So Charlie sits there and continues to mind his own
business, intent on his Tetris or Mario or whatever game he was playing. Ten minutes later, back comes Mrs. Monster.

MOM: Okay, I've got a snack for you: a Whopper with cheese, a
large order of onion rings, and a strawberry shake, just the way
you like it.

A snack? What do you suppose this woman gives this little tank
at mealtime?

CHARLIE: Okay, okay, I'll eat it, Mom. Lemme just finish my
game.

MOM: Charles, you put that game down right this instant and eat it before it gets cold. Besides, we're going to start boarding soon.

And so this little child was practically force-fed a sloppy, calorie-drunk fast-food orgy by a mother who didn't seem to recognize how she was turning her child into someone with a lifetime of weight problems.

Ultimately, we each must take responsibility for our own bodies. Don't misunderstand me: if this kid got a bad start in life in terms of diet and exercise, it's his responsibility to change once he escapes this woman's claws. Just as we parents must teach and warn our kids about the perils of smoking or drinking or reckless sexual behavior, we need to establish smart guidelines on proper nutrition at an early age.

The vast majority of overweight Americans are fat because we simply lack the willpower or courage or stamina to eat right. Once you do manage your body and lose weight and stay active, there is no greater feeling in the world. Having people compliment me on losing weight is a never-ending joy. You don't have to be a public person to enjoy those kinds of accolades. Believe me, everyone in your life will notice.

And let's not forget that vanity aside, losing weight will increase my chance of living a healthy, longer life. I want to be a thorn in the side of loony liberals for many, many years to come. If they're going to beat me, I don't want to lose because I dropped dead while trying to climb a flight of stairs.

Like most talk radio hosts, I receive lots of hate e-mail from critics. They often call me names like "right-wing nut," "Neocon," or "blowhard." They *used* to call me fat. Not anymore. On the rare occasions that I'd reply to one of these angry people, I'd say something like, "I may be fat but you're ugly. And I can always lose weight. But you're stuck." They'd usually get a kick out of that.

I turned out to be right. I can—and did—lose weight.

And they're still ugly.

# 15

# TO BE OR NOT TO BE . . . AN IDIOT

The thrust of the book that you now hold in your hands is political. True idiots, however, transcend political boundaries. They exist on the right, left and center. Believe me, I don't think I'm a snapshot of perfection. You can see that I've bared some of my faults, quirks, flaws and shortcomings in this book. I hope you also realize that I have some common sense and manners.

When I look around, it seems many people lack the basic prerequisites for getting along with others. Regardless of individual politics, everyone should agree that etiquette and decent behavior enhance our lives. Politeness and concern for others are sorely lacking in America today. Instead, the idiocy show intrudes on our lives.

After hearing from listeners for years, I've come up with a list of everyday displays of idiotic behavior that surrounds us.

## FAST FOOD WORKERS WHO BARELY SPEAK ENGLISH

This problem transcends the fast food industry. The refusal of immigrants to acclimate themselves to American culture is a maddening reality of twenty-first-century life in our country.

It feels as though this issue is spotlighted at the friendly neighborhood hamburger stand. Few people know fast food joints better than I do. Prior to losing weight, I was practically on a first-name basis with just about every Wendy's, McDonald's and Burger King in town. My routine was to eat lunch at one of these places four to five times a week, so I understand the frustration of trying to tell someone who barely speaks English how I don't want pickles on my burger. I've repeatedly been shortchanged, overcharged or charged for items that I didn't order. After all, how can someone who doesn't speak the language be expected to understand requests, fill orders or handle currency?

One night, my wife and I decided to order food from the new Chinese restaurant in town, Happy China. They offered free delivery, according to an ad in our local paper, and reviews praised their food. It was time to give them a try. I was the lucky one who offered to call and place the order. The conversation went something like this:

*(Ring, ring)*

HAPPY CHINA: Heh-yo, Hoppy China, yor ohdurh peez?

ME: I'd like two Sweet and Sour Chicken dinners, please.

HAPPY CHINA: Sweet suhr cheeken dinah? Wot kina rez?

ME: Excuse me?

HAPPY CHINA: Rez! Wot kina rez you wahnt?

ME: Rez? I'm sorry, I don't know what you're saying. Do I need to make a reservation? I don't want to come there, this is for delivery.

HAPPY CHINA: Rez! Rez! You wahnt fried or white rez?

ME: Oh, *rice!* I'm sorry, yes, we want fried rice, please.

HAPPY CHINA: Ah-dress?

ME: 100 Old Mill Lane.

HAPPY CHINA: Oluhd meel rode?

ME: Old Mill Lane.

HAPPY CHINA: Meel rode oloud?

ME: No, Old Mill Lane. Old Mill Lane. 100 Old Mill Lane.

HAPPY CHINA: Numbahr 100 Meel Olud Reever lane?

It was absolutely, positively hopeless. After five long minutes of this back and forth, me shouting, "100 Old Mill Lane" (Americans always yell when someone doesn't understand us, as if that helps) I finally piled into my car and drove, in the pouring rain, to Happy China Restaurant to pick up our food. The concept of delivery smashed on all those misunderstood words. I may have been in Happy China, but I was not a happy man.

This family of hardworking immigrants moved to the United States and opened a Chinese restaurant in a neighborhood full of English-speakers. The newcomers apparently applied for all the necessary permits, painted the walls, bought the equipment, ran some ads promoting the place—logical steps for anyone who wants to become an entrepreneur. So why isn't learning the language of their customers part of that business strategy?

Many of us had grandparents and great-grandparents who came to America from foreign lands with nothing more than a dream and a few clothes in their bags. They were proud to become Americans. They wanted to learn English, soak up the culture of their adopted country, acquire the skills needed to survive and succeed in their new homeland.

Today many immigrants create entire minicultures within their own neighborhoods. They refuse to learn English, yet expect to be treated exactly the same as other Americans. They are driving cars, operating machinery, and running restaurants without bothering to learn the language that the vast majority of us speak.

It's a shame.

If my wife and I decided to make a go of it in Czechoslovakia, we would know that learning the languages of that country would be part of our game plan. Welcome to America, Happy China owners. Now please learn English so you can figure out how to understand our address and find the homes of your other customers, too. We really do love your sweet and sour chicken.

It's just too much work to try and order it from you. Next time, I guess I'll have to take my chances at Burger King.

## WOMEN WHO MAKE A BIG PUBLIC DISPLAY OF BREAST-FEEDING THEIR BABIES

This strikes a nerve with many people.

First off, you have the wacky mothers who think it's perfectly logical to breast-feed a seven-year-old child in public. Once I interviewed one of these fanatics who gave a weird explanation of mother/child bonding for why women should be able to breast-feed children who are old enough to fix their own breakfasts. Then you have the women who flaunt breast-feeding in crowded places, like restaurants, shopping malls or department stores.

Criticize the older-child breast-feeders or the exhibitionists and certain feminists want you thrown in jail or worse. On the other side are people who think that women should never, ever breast-feed in public. They believe if a mother must choose between breast-feeding or going to the mall, she should stay home.

Once I watched in utter amazement as a woman came marching through a grocery store, baby clamped firmly on her breast. Mom was intent on filling the shopping list in her hand. She made no attempt whatsoever to cover her breast, so everyone in the grocery store essentially witnessed a topless show. This spectacle attracted a group of children, some as young as ten. They started following the woman and her baby through the aisles, giggling at the display of skin, seeing more flesh than any sex-education lesson would allow. With this entourage, the woman looked like a demented Pied Piper of breast-feeding. The look on her face said, "I just *dare* you to tell me I can't do what I'm doing."

I also rely on my wife's judgment about breast-feeding. After all, she had four little hungry boys to feed, at one point twins. Denise is very clear: "If you can tell that a woman is breast-feeding, she's doing it wrong. There's a way to do it with discretion so that the whole world doesn't have to watch. It's called 'draping.' "

So drape, or stay home or do it in the car in the parking lot. Breast-feeding is a private, intimate act and should remain that way.

## IDIOTS WHO TALK OUT LOUD IN MOVIE THEATERS

In what seems to be a new trend gaining momentum, rude moviegoers flaunt their complete and total lack of courtesy for others. Their annoying banter during showtime proves they are oblivious to the obvious: true movie fans, who have shelled out hard-earned cash to sit in a theater, have zero interest in hearing rambling conversations. They've paid to hear the actors on the big screen, not some chatterbox sitting in the audience.

Audience members, in growing numbers, seem compelled to blurt out whatever they're thinking right in the middle of the film. "Boy, Jim Carrey sure is a funny guy." "Look out, Spiderman, he's gonna sneak up from behind." "I think the wife is having an affair with the gardener and he killed the boyfriend." You've heard these loudmouths. They just can't seem to help themselves.

Maybe the popularity of home movie rentals is behind this regrettable phenomenon that is ruining theater outings with disturbing regularity. Families enjoy renting videotapes or DVDs, sitting in the den and watching—and talking—to their heart's content. For the life of me, I can't grasp why they forget that when they're out at the movies, away from the privacy of their homes, they need to shut their traps. These folks are total idiots and should be banished to an island somewhere in the Pacific. Better yet, make that an iceberg in the Arctic.

I've launched a one-man crusade against this form of rudeness. Recruits are welcome. Whenever someone blabs nonstop, even after others "shoosh" him, and it's obvious he's not going to stop, I slyly go to the concession stand, buy a bag of M&Ms and return, making sure I sit a couple of rows behind the loudmouth. When the culprit talks out loud, I plunk an M&M at his head.

This must be done carefully, with precise aim. After plunking the offender, you must look innocent, with no clue where the missile originated. It's an art form. So far, it has worked and they shut up. Not once has any chatterbox punched, stabbed, shot or even yelled at me.

Then again, I've never been caught. Yet.

## PEOPLE WHO WORK IN CUSTOMER SERVICE WHO SEEM TO HATE WORKING IN CUSTOMER SERVICE

This, too, is a pet peeve shared by many Americans. I call it the death of customer service in our country. And it's spiraling out of control.

When I was a little boy, my mom and dad owned two pizza parlors. I remember a sign that was hanging in the employees' break room: RULE NUMBER ONE: THE CUSTOMER IS ALWAYS RIGHT. RULE

NUMBER TWO: WHEN THE CUSTOMER IS WRONG, REFER TO RULE NUM-
BER ONE. My folks never forgot that customers were the reason they
were in business, kept the registers ringing and the bills paid.

Today a whole host of service industry workers, sales clerks,
phone operators, fast food employees, you name it, act as though the
customer is just a burden in their lives. We've all witnessed it: the
flight attendant who treats passengers like a bunch of intruders,
the utility company representative who is angry and disrespectful,
the Department of Motor Vehicles clerk so indifferent and unwilling
to help in any way, shape or form.

All of these bad-attitude, lazy workers share the same trait.
They're in a job, a chosen profession, called customer service *where
they have to work with customers.* Imagine that, working in a field
where you act as though you hate the reason you have a job: the customer.

My wife and I have experienced many situations where businesses lost our patronage forever over some relatively small transgres-
sion or issue. Like the time in a movie theater when the projector
broke down and we walked out—with management refusing to issue
a refund for our tickets. Bear in mind, we're not difficult people.
Quite the opposite. We just believe it's fair that when a company
screws up, it must offer to fix the problem, restore the item, and give
a refund, whatever, to satisfy the customer. If the company balks or
refuses, we're gone, never to return. They've just lost the Gallaghers,
reliable bill-paying consumers.

More and more people are taking this approach with rude, arrogant, nasty customer service representatives. Hey, there are a lot of
businesses and companies out there competing for our business.
Treated badly by one? Patronize another. Conversely, when you find

a company that treats customers properly, fairly and with respect, give them plenty of business and tell your friends. It's the best, and most satisfying, remedy.

## PARENTS WHO LET THEIR TEENAGERS GO TRICK-OR-TREATING

This seemingly minor infraction reveals a woeful lack of proper parenting skills. Our children aren't our buddies, our friends, or our brothers and sisters. We're the ones who must set ground rules and guidelines that teach our children how to become well-adjusted, considerate adults.

Today more and more parents are trying to win their children's acceptance. It's a disturbing trend that seems to be spreading. This faulty rationale has parents saying "yes" everytime, pacifying the kids with the hope this will make them behave.

I believe this mentality is behind the idiotic practice of teenagers going door-to-door at Halloween to get candy. It's a familiar sight in recent Halloweens. In the middle of cute little ghosts, goblins, and princesses stands some hulking, brooding sixteen- or seventeen-year-old, wearing no costume whatsoever, shifting back and forth on his or her feet, and embarrassingly saying, "trick or treat."

Parents should stop their teenagers from engaging in this kind of absurdity. Trick or treating is about the joy of youngsters getting dressed up, touring the neighborhood and returning home with a bag of goodies. High school juniors or seniors ruin the holiday when they glom onto the tradition just to feed their faces.

And Mom and Dad can just say "no."

## THE IDIOTIC EARLY DISPLAY OF CHRISTMAS LIGHTS AND DECORATIONS IN NEIGHBORHOODS

Retailers showcase Christmas decorations as early as possible because they're into sales and making money, so they figure that the sooner the holiday season starts, the more items they'll sell. I don't like the practice, but at least I understand it.

But I have no clue as to why homeowners and neighbors are rushing the holiday season, too. In the fall of 2004, several of our neighbors had Christmas lights up and on as early as the first of November. A couple of families even had their Christmas lights up and turned on the day after Halloween!

Folks have been complaining for decades about the commercialization of Christmas. I long for a time when we once again wait for Thanksgiving to pass before breaking out the Christmas decorations. That's the way it used to be and I have so many happy memories from those times. The rush to put up the tree and hang the lights makes us weary of Christmas by Christmas Eve. The season becomes so long, we can't wait for it to end. That's not the Christmas season I remember. Only after Thanksgiving did we dive in, decorate the house and tree, think about presents to give and revel in the blessings of the season.

Every time I've complained on-air about rushing Christmas, somebody inevitably calls in with explanations: they're leaving for much of December and want to enjoy the lights while they are still home, or they put the decorations up early to greet a relative returning from a long trip—all legitimate reasons. I'm just asking, on behalf of those of us who want to appreciate the season in its appropriate time, that people wait before turning on the lights until at least after Thanksgiving.

Let's return to cherishing every single day, every week of the holiday season. It's time to stop dragging it out for months.

## THE PEOPLE WHO DON'T KNOW HOW TO SAY "THANK YOU"

This one really bothers me.

Thank you. Two simple, special words that are so easy to say. For many misguided people, these words are impossible to utter.

A typical scene on an American street: a driver tries to exit a parking lot into slow-moving traffic. The motorist in the parking lot inches into the street, waiting, hoping for another driver who will let him in. I am almost always that obliging driver. A small favor like that feels good and it's so simple to help a stranger have an easier time navigating that sticky traffic moment. So I slow down, motion for the person to cut in front of me, and wait for the small gesture of appreciation to follow.

That gesture rarely comes.

I guess those drivers believe it's my duty to let them in; that it's their right to have someone acquiesce to their need to merge. Or maybe they just don't realize how rude it is not to thank, or even acknowledge, another driver who has just done them a favor, however small.

This sad phenomenon expands beyond driving. For example, it's frustrating to stand at a doorway, wait for someone behind you, and hold the door open only to watch that person stroll through without saying a single word.

We've strayed from so many basic common courtesies. Saying thank you was among the first casualties. It takes such little effort to wave, or just say thanks, after a total stranger treats you with respect.

I'm putting the world on notice: if these pinheads don't start saying thanks when I let them merge into traffic or when I hold open doors, I'm going to stop being Mr. Nice Guy. Forever.

That'll show 'em.

Thank you.

## TELEMARKETERS WHO WON'T TAKE "NO" FOR AN ANSWER

Telemarketing is a valid, legitimate way for companies to sell products or for marketing firms or pollsters to gauge public tastes and opinions. It's an essential cog in the machine we call capitalism.

In business, telemarketing works, it's a revenue behemoth. According to industry groups, telemarketers peddled $661 billion in goods and services to more than 180 million customers in 2001—a figure that represented nearly 6 percent of America's gross domestic product. So, there are folks who don't mind being cold-called. Most of us, however, dislike having the phone ring at dinnertime or when we're sitting down to watch a TV show or baseball game. That ringing phone is especially annoying when the caller tries to hawk us a vacuum cleaner or ask if the car dealership treated us well during the last service call.

In 2003, the Federal Trade Commission started the do-not-call registry. That way, if you don't want the bothersome calls, you can be removed from the phone lists telemarketers use. Certain nonprofits, charities, pollsters, politicians and firms already doing business with you can still call. Any other solicitor risks a $10,000 fine per unauthorized call. Withstanding court challenges, the list has soared to include about sixty-four million phone numbers by the fall of 2004, with millions more expected.

Even if you're on the do-not-call list, chances are you're going to get that call. Arguing with a telemarketer is becoming as inevitable as swatting away mosquitoes in the summer. They act boldly, approaching their tasks like Marines on a mission. Tell them that you're not interested; they just keep talking, intensifying their pitch. Say that you really have no need for the best new paint remover that has ever been invented, and they just keep trying to talk you into buying it.

Eventually, there's only one thing left to do: hang up on them. Most of us are extremely uncomfortable with doing that. It happens usually as a last resort, when you're so angry that only the slam of the receiver sends the clear message that this conversation is so over and must never start again.

There's just no need for a telemarketer to put someone in that sticky position. If they have alienated even people like me, who defend their profession, they must be crossing the line.

I'm an optimistic person. After a lifetime of ups and downs, I've gotten pretty adept at seeing the proverbial silver lining to every cloud. In listing these idiotic escapades, it dawns on me that this is all pretty depressing. I realize that a book called *Surrounded by Idiots: Fighting Liberal Lunacy in America* will by definition be a collection of opinions and behaviors that make us crazy.

Keeping with my spirit of trying to find the best in life, I have another list. These are people who are definitely *not* idiots. They are the kinds of people who keep our country great, the neighbor you cherish or the wonderful coworker you remember. They're the people who keep us sane, who balance the idiocy in America with kindness, common sense and goodness.

## NEIGHBORS WHO WELCOME NEWCOMERS TO THE COMMUNITY

Bringing a pie or a plate of cookies to a new family who just moved into your neighborhood used to be as common as church on Sunday. For some reason, those days are long gone.

My family and I have moved into new neighborhoods about half a dozen times over the past dozen years. I can count on one hand the times when a neighbor came by to welcome us with the once-prevalent gesture of bringing by some goodies.

We don't have some freakish sweet tooth nor are we too cheap to buy or make our own pie. It's just that a move is a traumatic, major life event and it sure is nice when a new neighbor greets you with a sample of good home-cooking.

When we moved into our present house, I had pretty much given up. No way would anyone bother stopping by to say hello. People just don't do that anymore, I guess, so there was no point in expecting it. As soon as the moving van left, though, a middle-aged couple rang our doorbell and welcomed us to the neighborhood. They brought a plate of chocolate chip cookies. I knew I was going to love this place. Sure enough, it's the best neighborhood we've ever lived in.

Recently, a young family moved into the house next door and we passed on the tradition. Denise whipped up her famous brownies. We brought them over and said, "Welcome to the neighborhood." When the mother answered our knock on her door, her face had a weary look that translated as "I'm tired and cranky and can't believe we've just been through this experience." As soon as she saw our smiling faces and the plate of brownies (which her three little boys probably devoured in minutes), her face lit up and she seemed relieved to know that nice people lived next door.

Well, we're nice most of the time.

So take a few minutes and greet someone who is moving into your neighborhood. It really does a world of good and is an easy way to make new neighbors feel welcome and appreciated.

## PEOPLE WHO GIVE MONEY TO HOMELESS STREET PEOPLE

Okay, have you keeled over in disbelief? Are you frozen in shock? Are you surprised that an avowed conservative believes in giving money to panhandlers?

Step into my mind here for a minute. Not too long ago, I refused, on principle, to give them money. Like many, I figured that most street people just wanted cash for drugs or booze. They didn't really want to WORK FOR FOOD nor were they HUNGRY AND NEED A MEAL as their cardboard signs said. To me, they seemed like drug addicts trying to score another fix.

That all changed one day while waiting for a train in the crowded, bustling Penn Station in New York City. I was engaged in my usual hobby of watching all the colorful characters pass by when I saw a shabbily dressed woman standing outside a McDonald's. With her were her children, four little ragamuffins who looked like characters from a Charles Dickens novel, wearing dirty, torn clothes and beat-up, worn shoes. They were all begging from the commuters walking briskly by.

"Please help us," they'd say. "We are so hungry, we haven't eaten all day and we badly need something to eat." Like me, most of the passersby were ignoring them. It's a lot easier to dismiss people like this than to interact with them. "Please, mister, we're homeless and we are living in a park, but we have no food and we're *so* hungry."

Finally, a middle-aged businessman with briefcase in hand stopped and gave the family some money. The mother and children were so grateful, their faces lit up with big smiles. "Thank you, sir. God bless you for your kindness." Immediately, the mother took her four little ones into the restaurant and ordered food for them. I noticed that the money they had been given couldn't buy enough food for all five of them. So the mother acted like any good mom: she went without and made sure her children ate. She seemed so happy to be able to put some food in her babies' mouths.

I had my epiphany. Watching that businessman take a second and give that woman a few dollars, I saw how a person who is lucky enough to have a nice life managed to share some of his good fortune with someone who had nothing except the love shared with her children. God bless Good Samaritans.

I realized that a dollar, or two, or five might not mean much to you and me, but it could be a windfall for a needy person, buy a long overdue meal or a night out of the cold. I went into the restaurant and gave the woman money so she could buy herself food. I felt terrific as I walked away. Today, I try not to stop and think about how the person begging will spend the money I give them.

It took a little nerve for me to admit on the radio that I had started giving handouts to street people. A lot of folks who call themselves conservatives were angry with me. They said I was just contributing to the welfare state, that I was enabling drug users, blah blah blah.

An e-mail I received from a guy in Iowa made it all worthwhile:

Mike, three years ago, a man with a "will work for food" sign came up to my car. I knew about a construction company that was looking for menial laborers. I gave him a buck and told him about the work site. He immediately went down there, got a job, and is now a division manager of that same company, overseeing a whole team of construction workers.

E. L.

Giving, with no strings attached, to a homeless person is a great feeling that lasts a long time. Try it, you'll see what I mean.

## PARENTS WHO AREN'T AFRAID TO DISCIPLINE THEIR CHILDREN

Our kids always complained that they had it rough growing up, that as parents we were too strict. Our sons were not allowed to party all night God knows where, like some of their high school pals. Denise and I did our best to always make sure we knew where they were. If we didn't like the sound of the places they were headed, if the event sounded dicey or totally unsupervised, then they had to stay home.

If one of our sons did something that deserved punishment, he was punished. We tried to be consistent in grounding them if they broke an ironclad rule. It was one of the many ways we tried to teach them that actions have consequences. Denise and I also constantly remind our children how much we love them, how much pride and happiness they give us. We praise them for trying hard in school and let them know how grateful we are to have such good kids. Our love for them never made us afraid to discipline them when they needed it. That's the way it was in our home.

Today, fewer and fewer parents seem willing to be tough with their children. My wife and I believe that many parents today are foolishly hell-bent on being their children's "friend." I have no idea why this attitude is so pervasive, but you see it all the time. I was floored when a lady called me once on the air to brag about a new parents' group she was forming.

The conversation went like this:

ME: Jenny, you're on the *Mike Gallagher Show*.

JENNY: Mike, thanks for taking my call. I disagree with you about the need for parents being tougher on their kids. We have rising drug rates, teenage pregnancy out of control, kids are just off the deep end. Clearly, your approach doesn't work.

ME: Okay, so if my way doesn't work, what do you think is the solution?

JENNY: I was hoping you'd ask *(laughter)*. Mike, a couple of friends of mine and I are forming a group called MADF.

ME: MADF? I'm almost afraid to ask, Jenny.

JENNY: MADF stands for Moms are our daughters' friends.

ME: You've *got* to be kidding me.

JENNY: No, I'm not. We're a group of concerned parents and we really think we're onto something big here.

ME: Well, for starters, you oughta get your organization's name right—if it's "Moms are our daughters' friends" that'd be MAODF, not MADF . . .

JENNY: That's not important, Mike.

ME: Clearly.

JENNY: Joke all you want. We are relating to our daughters as their peers, as a way to see the world through their eyes. Kids have it tough these days, Mike, you just have no idea. And so we're relating to our children a lot better than I'll bet you or your wife relate to *your* children.

MADF, indeed. Should be MAD, as in idiotic. This well-meaning, well-intentioned dingbat of a parent thinks that the way to get her daughter to behave is to be her buddy, her peer. Sadly, I think Jenny just expresses what a lot of misguided moms and dads are thinking and doing. They believe that parenting will be easier if they can get their child to like them as a friend.

Wrong. Children need limits and parents must set them, which means acting like a policeman, not a friend, at times. I didn't mean to be crass, but I think my final advice to Jenny was true:

ME: Get ready for a world of anxiety, Jenny. I'll bet it'll be no time before your daughter is wearing nose rings, has her backside tattooed, and is stoned out of her mind on a regular basis.

I hope, for Jenny's sake, that I'm wrong. But I doubt it.

## POLITE TEENAGERS

I love meeting kids from the South. I'm sure that kids from the North, East or West have wonderful parents who have also taught their children manners.

However, hear a teen call you "sir" or "ma'am," and chances are that he or she hails from Dixie. Southerners teach basic etiquette to children from an early age. For these children, "sir or ma'am" is the automatic greeting for an adult. Opening up a door for a woman is standard procedure. So is standing tall and firmly shaking the hand of a man they are meeting.

Traveling across the country, I meet families all the time. Usually it's the moms and dads who listen to my radio show or watch me on Fox while their kids have absolutely no idea what I do, they're just along for the ride. It's always a joy to meet a young person who is polite and well mannered. Based on my experiences, many parents are doing a good job—and not all of them are from the South.

But sometimes, a child's good manners can get him or her into trouble.

In 1994, I moved Denise and our four boys from South Carolina to upstate New York. We were to experience huge culture shock, and one evening as I returned home from work, Denise greeted me with a worried look. My heart sank. Seemed that Trevor, our second oldest who was around fifteen at the time, was in trouble at school.

"Mrs. Wach called and said that Trevor was being sarcastic, rude, and disruptive in her class," Denise told me. "We've got to have a parent-teacher conference tomorrow afternoon."

Great. An emergency parent-teacher conference called by the teacher. Ranks right up there with root canal, in my book. But the next day, off we went.

Grumpy, humorless Mrs. Wach tore right into us.

"Trevor is simply annoying and sarcastic," she said forcefully. "His sarcasm is constantly turning the other children against me and I don't like it one little bit."

Sarcastic didn't sound like our Trevor. He could be playful and rambunctious but hardly ever sarcastic.

"Mrs. Wach," I sheepishly asked, "what's he doing that's so sarcastic?"

"It's very simple," she said. "My class is very interactive and I call on students quite frequently. Every time I call on Trevor, he calls me 'ma'am.'"

"Yes?"

"Well, that's it; he is constantly ridiculing me by calling me 'ma'am.' I just won't have it!"

"Is he saying it in a nasty tone of voice, or in a smart-aleck way?" Denise asked.

"He doesn't have to," this miserable excuse of a teacher answered. "No teenager says 'ma'am' and you both know it."

"Well our son does," I said.

Mrs. Wach just didn't get it and we arranged to transfer Trevor from her class. He went on to earn a B+ in the course. It had been some utterly forgettable, boring class that had been taught by an utterly forgettable, boring teacher named Mrs. Wach (not her real name, by the way).

For his good grade, we took Trevor to Dairy Queen for a big hot fudge sundae. We were also glad he treated a teacher, even a dope like Mrs. Wach, with respect. It's great when your kid makes you proud.

## SENIOR CITIZEN COUPLES WHO STILL HOLD HANDS

I treasure my marriage to Denise because our relationship has made my life rich and fulfilling. I'm sorry for people who are going through life alone. If that's you, I hope and pray that you will someday find someone who will bring you as much joy as my wife brings me.

For the first year we were married, I was uncomfortable with expressing affection for Denise in public. Kissing her in front of anyone else was out of the question. Holding hands in public was just not going to happen. The best I could manage was holding the door open for her or pulling back her chair when we sat down at a restaurant.

About a year after we were married, I read about a guy somewhere in the Midwest who had lost his wife to cancer. In the seven years since she had died, he still mourned her every day. Worst of all, he regretted all the times he hadn't been affectionate with her. His quote stuck with me: "I acted like such a macho jerk that I wouldn't even hold her hand when she wanted to," he said. "I'd give anything to have her back just so I could show her that I'd be willing to hold her hand."

That story broke my heart. Since then, I enjoy walking hand-in-hand with Denise. I reach for my wife's hand in public as much as possible. I'm no longer shy about showing my feelings. Sometimes, I wonder if our love will always be this affectionate. I think about what our lives will be like twenty or thirty years from now (God willing). Will we still hold hands?

It's always heartwarming to see a couple of senior citizens who still hold hands. They look so happy together, like they're just so grateful to have another day in each other's company. I know I'm grateful for every day I have with my Denise. I hope I'm holding her hand till my dying day.

## AMERICANS WHO STILL FLY THE FLAG

Why does it take an act of terror on United States soil to display the American flag?

In the days and weeks after 9/11, Old Glory appeared everywhere. It seemed like every car had a flag attached. Millions of Americans proudly flew the flag outside their homes, an act of unity that said, "We're all in this together." Sadly, we saw fewer and fewer displays of Old Glory as time went by. I guess people just got tired of going through the effort.

Pity.

Down the street from our home, a senior citizen named Jack flies the American flag morning, noon, and night. He even installed a little floodlight to illuminate it at night, following the protocol of not flying the flag in the dark. I've seen him out in front of his house in the rain running the flag up his pole or back down again. He never misses a day. When he goes out of town, he pays a neighborhood kid to make sure his flag is always on display.

I often stop and talk to him when I'm out walking the dogs.

He's as delightful a guy as you'll ever meet. Once, I asked him about his dedication and determination to fly that flag.

"We're at war, Mike," he said. "And as a World War II vet, it hurts to see how few Americans seem to think that it matters to fly the flag. It does matter. It matters to the families of those who are serving, it matters to those of us who love our country, it matters to every man, woman and child who knows how great it feels to put patriotism on display."

Putting patriotism on display. I like that.

As someone who spends a considerable amount of time on TV, I made it a point to wear an American flag lapel pin on camera when the war began. I figured that could be my small reminder that lots of us love our country and aren't afraid to show it.

And then, ABC-TV made an idiotic decision forbidding its anchors and reporters from wearing American flags or patriotic ribbons on the air. The network said they were protecting the objectivity of their reporters.

"What if Peter's wearing one, but Ted's not? Does that mean one journalist is more patriotic than the other? It's best not to place such an unfair burden on the reporters," said ABC spokesman Jeffrey Schneider (to the Cox News Service), referring to Peter Jennings and Ted Koppel.

"We cannot signal through outward symbols how we feel, even if the cause is justified. Overseas, it could be perceived that we're just mouthpieces for the U.S. government, and that can place our journalists in danger," Schneider said.

When I heard that an American television network would actually make it a point to forbid its on-air talent from wearing a flag lapel pin, I made a vow. I would never, ever appear on TV without one.

Except for one mix-up with my suit at the dry cleaners, I've always done so.

I love seeing people like Jack display the American flag. Here's hoping for a return to the days when patriotism was in style.

## BOSSES WHO REMEMBER TO COMPLIMENT THEIR EMPLOYEES

There must be a "boss school" that managers attend in secret. What else can explain the universal failure of many bosses to give their employees a kind word or two?

In my career, I've worked for a lot of bosses. All of them—men and women, young and old, and white and black—shared the same trait: a reluctance to give anyone who worked for them kudos for a job well done. It's an unfair management style, inflicted on plenty of folks in the American workforce. You bust your fanny for a company, and you usually get a "what will you be doing for us tomorrow?" kind of reception.

No wonder so many labor disputes erupt in our country. With bosses unwilling to let an employee know that he or she is doing a good job, it's easy to understand what leads to the feeling that it's us versus them, the little guy against the big, bad company.

I currently have a boss who goes out of his way to thank his employees and let them know when they've done a good job. Yet even Greg Anderson, the president of the Salem Radio Network, admits it isn't easy.

"I always came from the school that says if you give too many compliments or plaudits to people, they'll eventually stop producing results," he once told me. "Believe me, some of the best managers in

America follow that line of thinking. But over the years, I came to the conclusion that employees should be treated the way I would want to be treated."

It's great to work for someone with that attitude. As companies continue to phase out unions, that kind of enlightened management style will be needed to boost morale and keep employees happy.

This isn't to say that bosses should just dole out compliments unnecessarily; there's no merit or wisdom in gratuitous, empty pleasantries. But if you're a boss and your employee does a good job, tell him or her.

They'll be willing to go through a brick wall for you.

## EMPLOYEES WHO ARE LOYAL TO THEIR COMPANY

Many Americans suffer from what I call the "union mentality," an eagerness to do everything in their power to shortchange their employer.

They take the maximum amount of sick days, try to extend the coffee break or lunch break, or just put in the minimum amount of work each day that they can get away with. These people act like it's a huge burden to even show up. These are not my kind of people.

My kind of people are those who appreciate being on "the team." These are employees who realize that if the company succeeds, in most cases they will be rewarded. They understand and appreciate the value of teamwork and will strive to make their office, their factory, their radio station, their company become the absolute best in the business.

That attitude makes all the difference. It can turn people from hating their job into loving their work. The best advice I've heard was, "Go out and find a job you love and you'll never work a day in your life."

Even if you don't love your job, celebrate simply because you have work. Stand out in the crowd, go the extra mile. It may not feel like it, but you'll win in the long run. And you'll be happier than ever.

Despite the title of this book, plenty of people excel, strive to help others, and make this world a better place. In fact, the list of *non*-idiots could go on and on.

A good friend of mine, who happens to be my church pastor, once told a story about his Sunday school children. It's a lesson that can apply to people of all ages:

"When I teach young children, I often use the half-glass full of water as a way to introduce some Bible lessons," said Dr. John McKellar of White's Chapel United Methodist Church in Southlake, Texas. "I hold up the glass that's half-filled and I ask them, 'Is this glass half full or half empty? Inevitably, the children say both—some of the kids say half full, others say half empty. Which is just what I want them to say.

"I tell them that they're all correct. The glass is both: it's half full *and* half empty at all times. And what really matters is how you look at the glass. If you look at the glass as half full, you're the kind of person that God expects, a person with an optimistic, positive outlook on life who is ready to go out in the world and do good things for others."

It's a great lesson. We should all be like those children in John's Sunday school class, full of questions and wonderment but willing to accept sage advice. And our eyes open to all the good things in life, even at the worst times.

# 16

# THERE'S STILL REASON TO HOPE

By its nature, talk radio splits the world into black and white and doesn't see shades of gray. There's right and wrong, good versus bad, truth and light arrayed against murky propaganda and deceit.

While it's my job to spotlight problems and keep my radar attuned to those pesky liberals, the world outside the broadcasting booth can be more balanced, more positive, than a daily rant might suggest. Much good happens in this great country of ours. All is not lost. Lately, we have been witnessing some wonderful developments. The election of 2004 proved to be a triumph of red states over blue. Voters repudiated the slippery slope of declining morals and out-of-touch liberal politicians. A cultural revolution has been dramatically curtailing the spread of indecent material over the free and public airwaves. Judges willing to acknowledge faith-based ideologies have been allowed to sit on the bench. There's even been talk of one day overturning *Roe v. Wade* and acknowledging abortion on demand to be a gross and pitiful loss of life.

The question of unity remains. Can we ever become a united people, put our differences behind us, enjoy the fruits of our nation and live in peace and freedom, as the founding fathers had hoped? Early in this book, I introduced my wife, Denise, who grounds me and gives me much joy and happiness. She is patient and kind, a wonderful wife, a terrific mother and a Democrat.

It's not always easy living with one. We rarely agree on political matters, and often argue about the direction of our country and the leaders who guide us. But if Denise wasn't in my life, I'd probably be filled with despair and anger for those opposed to the politically conservative world where I make my living. It would be easy to dismiss Democrats as a bunch of liberal idiots set wildly apart from mainstream American values and standards that so many of us cherish.

American people aren't as simple as that. Our people, our culture, our beliefs reflect those varying shades of gray in the real world. Most Americans don't follow their chosen political party lock, stock and barrel. Not every Democrat is a lost cause.

Take a look at the following quote and you'll see what I mean.

Now, don't get me wrong, the people I meet in small towns and big cities and diners and office parks, they don't expect government to solve all of their problems. They know they have to work hard to get ahead. And they want to. Go into the blue collar counties around Chicago and people will tell you: They don't want their tax money wasted by a welfare agency or by the Pentagon.

Go into any inner-city neighborhood, and folks will tell you that government alone can't teach kids to learn. They know that parents have to teach, that children can't achieve unless we raise their expectations and turn off the television sets and eradicate the slander that says a black youth with a book is acting white. They know those things.

Does that sound like a liberal lunatic? When Barack Obama said those words during his keynote speech at the 2004 Democratic National Convention, a political star was born. He went on to be elected U.S. Senator from Illinois. Time will tell if he meets or exceeds his party's expectations and the hopes of people in Illinois and beyond.

While he toes the party line on many political and ideological issues, he strikes me as the kind of politician who can appeal to both Democrats and Republicans. Instead of wallowing in hate and angry rhetoric, Barack Obama is a Democrat who challenges people to be their best, who speaks of hope and optimism rather than fear and despair.

Despite his place on the wrong side of the political fence, I like the guy. He's the kind of Democrat who represents the best in his party's future. He sure beats the likes of Ted Kennedy, Robert Byrd, John Kerry, Hillary Clinton, et al. I believe it's possible to appreciate other viewpoints and understand perspectives that differ from our own. It's just that many Democrats today don't give conservatives like me much to work with. Instead of Barack Obama's optimism, they wallow in the pessimism and anger of folks like Michael Moore.

People often ask how in the world I could be happily married to a Democrat. Sometimes this question is asked harshly and with venom, which once happened to Denise and me at a church party, of all places.

We're active in our Methodist church where Denise is a Stephen's Minister, a layperson who counsels people suffering through traumatic and challenging times. She trained extensively for this counseling work, once again making me awfully proud of her.

One evening at a church gathering, a man approached, congratulating me on my radio show and my conservative views. Then he began picking on Denise. "How can you live with that wife of yours?" he asked. To her face, he started insulting her: "How can you possibly be a member of our church with your goofy liberal views? Since you're a Democrat, your children are going to grow up to rape and pillage, they're going to become degenerates. You're completely immoral."

Before I could set him straight, Denise, no wilting wallflower, did a fine job in defending herself. I shouldn't have been surprised. She patiently and calmly explained how right and wrong doesn't have to be defined by political boundaries; that she didn't consider herself a bad person, least of all a degenerate, because of her political views. And she sweetly told him how sorry she was for people who saw the world that way.

Yet I know why that guy blasted her. After all, I make my living on radio and TV by verbally taking apart "the other side." If my marriage to the greatest woman in the world has taught me anything, it's that not all Democrats are misguided morally ambiguous villains. Denise has the biggest heart of anyone I've ever met and I know she means well, even if many of her political views are so wrong (sorry, honey).

If Denise and I can enjoy a strong, happy marriage, Republicans and Democrats can live and work together. We need to try and focus on what we share, rather than on what tears us apart. Because we're all Americans.

Remember what it felt like to be united after 9/11? Petty differences, political infighting and partisan lobbying crumbled in the face of our common need to join as one and fight our enemies. We grieved together as one nation, under God. It shouldn't take a terrorist attack to reunite us again. All of us, Republicans, Democrats, active political types or passive apolitical citizens, should take a deep breath and try to at least understand the other side. We should remember that a chosen political party doesn't always define a person's heart and soul.

Don't think I've lost my mind. I'm not suggesting that we forego our beliefs and ideas. But at a time when the world has grown so dangerous and we've become the target of hideous terrorists, we need to be unified, now more than ever. Our sons, daughters and grandchildren will go out into the world and freely choose their political party, what role they'll play and how active they'll be in the political process.

For their sakes, we should be an example, show them a loving heart and a principled spirit. We need to understand the art of compromise, which President Bush has practiced for years now, without abandoning our core beliefs and values.

I bellow about being surrounded by idiots realizing that many of those idiots think that I'm one, too. While I may tweak, tease, poke and prod in my ongoing campaign to be a thorn in the side of all Democrats and liberals, I remember that my criticisms target not an enemy but fellow Americans. I'm debating someone's wife or husband, son or daughter, or mother or father. I try to remind myself that just because they're Democrats, that doesn't give them a black heart or an empty soul.

Sunshine can spread. A fair share of listeners, many former life-long Democrats, have called my radio show or written me saying that I've managed to convert them to the Republican side.

Who knows, maybe someday, there'll be hope for Denise. And me.

God bless America.

# ACKNOWLEDGMENTS

As a first-time author, I found that trying to thank all the people in my life who have helped me with this book or my career is a daunting task. Like most of us, I've been blessed with so many individuals who have helped me along the way that it's impossible to list them all. Forgive me.

Of course, my world is my family: my wife, Denise, and our sons, Bryan, Trevor, Matt, and Micah. They've loved, accepted, and supported me no matter what. They've been uprooted from South Carolina to New York to Texas without saying a peep. No matter what the peaks and valleys, I've always been able to count on my family. They've made me the luckiest, happiest man in the universe.

The idea of writing a book was Larry Kramer's. He's a first-class manager who has done more for my career in a few years than I've managed to accomplish in twenty-seven.

Thanks to the William Morrow team, especially editor Mauro DiPreta. His faith and confidence, not to mention his reliably insightful pencil notes in the margins, gave me inspiration.

Alice McQuillan was an invaluable asset in helping me get to the finished product. Her title might be "book doctor," but she is really more of a miracle worker.

And literary agent Dan Strone is one of the best in the business. His patience and kindness in guiding this rookie through his first book was wonderful.

As to broadcasting, thanks to all the bosses who have hired me over the past nearly three decades.

To my first radio boss, Chris Mitchell, who hired a wet-behind-the ears, seventeen-year-old kid at WAVI in Dayton, Ohio, in 1978; to the late Johnny Walker of WKEF-TV, also in Dayton, who gave me my first TV job.

Thanks to Mike Scinto, a talented radio host and good friend who was instrumental in helping me advance in my radio career.

To Jim Burnside, the WFBC/Greenville, South Carolina, program director whose hiring of me allowed me to return to the world of talk radio after an ill-fated couple of years as a TV sportscaster.

To Larry Gorick, whose recommendation to Tom Parker and Michael Whalen at WGY/Albany, New York, landed me that gig just two hours north of the big city; to Frank Raphael, who heard me on WGY and recommended me to the WABC program director.

To Phil Boyce, John McConnell, Tim McCarthy and Mitch Dolan of WABC/New York for their kindness and guidance in teaching me the ropes of big-time radio.

To John Dame and his father Al, whose faith in my work led to the national launch of the Mike Gallagher radio show; to Greg Anderson, my mentor and boss who continued my national radio show by bringing it into the Salem Radio Network fold.

To Roger Ailes at Fox News Channel, one of the true broadcasting geniuses of the twenty-first century. His vision will be felt for decades. It's gratifying to see someone accomplish so much and do it with grace and style. Thanks to him and two other class acts at Fox, Kevin Magee and Bill Shine, for continuing to allow a guy like me with a face made for radio to do my thing on their airwaves.

Also, huge kudos to the fantastic bunch who works behind the scenes to make the radio show run so smoothly: director of operations Eric Hansen, producer Jason Hiatt, Derek Anderson, Linnae Young, Margaret Regan, Carolyn Feleo, Bonnie Simmonds, Charley Mefferd, Sherrod Munday, Bob Belt, Tom Tradup, Tyler Cox and everyone on the terrific team at Salem Radio Network.

Thanks to Tom Bigby and Jerry Bobo at KRLD/Dallas for having the faith to give me a big break in the city I call home.

To my dear friend Peter Rief, the show's creative services director and announcer, who is like a brother to me. It's his booming voice and creative spirit that give the radio show such a distinctive sound. But it's his friendship that means the most.

Thanks to my buddy Sean Hannity, whose wonderful foreword to this book gives you an idea why he has enjoyed a meteoric rise in radio and television. It's fun to watch good things happen to good people like him.

Most of all, thanks to you for listening to the radio show, watching Fox News Channel, or picking up this book. We may not always agree and you might not always like what I have to say, but I'll never lose sight of the fact that your support has made it possible for me to do what I love all these years. For that, I'll always be grateful.